THE
OPEN DOOR LANGUAGE SERIES
Second Book — Better Everyday English

BY

ZENOS E. SCOTT

Superintendent of Schools, Springfield, Massachusetts; formerly Assistant Commissioner in Charge of Elementary Education, State of New Jersey, and Superintendent of Schools, Trenton, New Jersey, and Louisville, Kentucky

RANDOLPH T. CONGDON

Principal of the State Normal School, Potsdam, New York; formerly Supervisor of English, State of New York

HARRIET E. PEET

Research Scholar in Education, Cambridge, Massachusetts; formerly Teacher in the Chicago Public Schools and in the State Normal School, Salem, Massachusetts

AND

LAURA FRAZEE

Assistant Superintendent, Primary Grades and Kindergarten, Baltimore, Maryland; formerly Supervising Principal, Demonstration and Practice School, Western Kentucky State Normal School, Bowling Green, Kentucky, and Assistant Superintendent of Schools, Indianapolis, Indiana

HOUGHTON MIFFLIN COMPANY

BOSTON · NEW YORK · CHICAGO · DALLAS · SAN FRANCISCO

The Riverside Press Cambridge

ACKNOWLEDGMENT

The authors of this text wish to express their appreciation of the generosity of the following publishers in allowing them to use their copyrighted selections: to The Copp Clark Co., Limited, Toronto, for "The Quarrel," "A Crafty Fox," "Tabby's Moving Day," and "A Brave Dog," from *Stories and Outlines for Composition*, by W. J. Karr; to Dodd, Mead & Co. for "An Encounter with Bears," from *Christopher Carson*, by John S. C. Abbott; to Everybody's Magazine, for "A Dizzy Climb," adapted from *The Heroes of the Gunnison Tunnel*, by A. W. Rolker and Day Allen Willey; to Houghton Mifflin Co. for "Little Jack Sparrow," from *Nights with Uncle Remus*, by Joel Chandler Harris, "John Muir," adapted from the *Introduction* to *Stickeen*, and for selections by Mary Carolyn Davies, Olive Thorne Miller, John Fiske, John Muir, Celia Thaxter, and Maurice Thompson; to Lothrop, Lee & Shepard Co. for a selection by Emilie Poulsson; to The Macmillan Company, for selections on pages 147, 148, 218 and 220 from Tarr and McMurry's Complete Geography; and to James T. White & Co. for a selection by Lydia Coonley Ward.

The Riverside Press

CAMBRIDGE · MASSACHUSETTS

PRINTED IN THE U.S.A.

FOREWORD

Purpose. This book is intended for the fifth and sixth grades in the elementary school. It endeavors to aid pupils during these formative years in establishing habits of thought and expression that will prove of permanent value.

Standards of accomplishment. These grades mark the transition from the spontaneous use of language, characteristic of early childhood, to the reticent period that precedes adolescence. Since it is a time of breaking away from the old and of preparing for the new, the work should be in close sympathy with children and of such a nature as to include a vision of the future. The standards of accomplishment used as a basis for the present text were derived from an extensive study of what children at this stage of development try to do. The book endeavors to meet the needs revealed and otherwise to be genuinely helpful to the pupils.

Better everyday English. In order to carry out the spirit of the title, the book lays particular emphasis on those aspects of English that are essential to everyday intercourse. It provides a thorough training in conversation, oral composition, and letter-writing.

Close relation to other school subjects. The book supplies exercises in learning how to study and in preparing topical recitations. It thus points the way to bringing the work in English into close relation with other school subjects.

Thorough training in correct usage. By recurrent cumulative tests and practice exercises, the book provides a thorough training in correct usage. The tests enable the pupils to find out what errors need correction; the practice exercises help them to master the correct forms.

Adaptation of work to pupils varying in ability and type of mind. All pupils are encouraged to find their own tasks, but this book, as well as the others in the series, frequently suggests work of three grades: one type that appeals to immature and less imaginative pupils; a second type that appeals to the creative instinct of pupils near the class median in ability; and a third type that calls forth the initiative and thought power of the most advanced pupils. By this plan each pupil, while working on the highest level of his ability, is able to undertake tasks that are both appealing and profitable.

Self-help. Finally, in order that pupils may gain independence in their work, the book provides (1) a summary of the points by which pupils may check their work; (2) a composition scale by which they may measure their compositions; and (3) a program for individual progress in form study and correct usage. This last feature is provided so that in small classes where it is desired pupils may work independently, each progressing at his own rate of speed.

BRIEF SUGGESTIONS TO TEACHERS

Encourage pupils to take initiative in the work and to feel responsibility for their own progress. Use the tests and the composition score to help them in measuring their work.

See that the work in conversation and composition is done under the stimulus of communicating ideas, but prevent aimless talking. Each lesson should be both an expression of thought and a training in form.

In conducting a lesson, follow the plan used by the book. Encourage first a free, spontaneous expression of ideas; and then, as the discussion proceeds, help the pupils to organize their ideas in such a way that they can sum them up in informal talks. Throughout the work help the pupils to realize that the foundation of all effective use of language is clear thinking.

Have all the pupils take part in the work; and, without mentioning the difference in their ability, see that each one is kept working at his highest level.

Endeavor to have all criticism positive rather than negative. Lay the emphasis on what should be done rather than on what should be avoided.

See that courtesy prevails at all times and that pupils are kept simple and honest. All work of the imagination should be labeled as such.

TABLE OF CONTENTS

PART ONE

AIMS. 1. To impress pupils with the fact that all clear expression depends upon clear thinking. 2. To aid pupils in forming such habits as: (a) speaking courteously and correctly; (b) composing all talks before giving them; (c) expressing ideas in clear sentences free from affectation; (d) choosing appropriate words; (e) using an agreeable voice and enunciating clearly; (f) writing papers that are neat in appearance and correct in form; (g) "proof-reading" all written work.

CHAPTER I — TELLING STORIES ENTERTAININGLY

CHAPTER II — SCHOOL NEWS

CHAPTER III — GOOD TIMES READING

CHAPTER IV — STORIES OF DOGS AND OTHER PETS

CHAPTER V — FAMOUS PICTURES AND STORIES

CHAPTER VI — HOME OCCUPATIONS AND ENTERPRISES

CHAPTER VII — CURIOUS HOMES

CHAPTER VIII — THE STORY OF THE AMERICAN FLAG

PART TWO

Aims. 1. To bring the study of English into effective relation with other school subjects. 2. To aid pupils in cultivating the following habits: (a) of talking and writing with the point of view of an audience in mind; (b) of organizing a theme around a central thought and of thinking it out with a plan in mind; (c) of expressing ideas in clear, well-formed sentences; (d) of showing some discrimination in the use of words; (e) of writing papers that are neat in appearance and correct in form; (f) of proof-reading all written work; (g) of being self-critical.

CHAPTER I — IMPROVING OUR EVERYDAY SPEECH

CHAPTER II — MAKING A TALK INTERESTING

TABLE OF CONTENTS

CHAPTER VIII — USEFUL OCCUPATIONS

CHAPTER IX — A GUIDE TO CORRECT USAGE

BETTER EVERYDAY ENGLISH
PART ONE

FOREWORD TO BOYS AND GIRLS

In a story in the Arabian Nights Ali Baba learns a charm that opens the door into a cave filled with treasure. He has but to say two words and the door flies open, and he is able to carry away with him bags of silver and gold and precious jewels.

We should all of us like to find an open door to treasure. We may not wish so much for gold and jewels, but we all desire a wealth of friends, a wealth of happiness, and a wealth of the satisfaction that comes from being of use in the world.

By helping you to think clearly and to talk and write entertainingly, this book endeavors to open the door for you to such treasure.

SECOND BOOK

BETTER EVERYDAY ENGLISH — PART ONE

Chapter I

TELLING STORIES ENTERTAININGLY

1. Fun in Carrying Out a Plan

[Conversation]

1. Most boys and girls enjoy making something out of scraps of material that they have at hand. Out of pieces of old lumber a clever boy will make a little sailboat, a bow and arrow, the frame for a kite, or he may even build a playhouse. From the contents of a rag bag a clever girl will create really beautiful clothes for her doll.

2. During your vacation you have had time to work out ideas that other boys and girls will like to hear about. Perhaps you have been as clever as Ralph, the boy who built the engine shown in the picture. Name something that you have made and then study the picture to find how Ralph built his engine.

3. If you were to complete the following story using only a few sentences, what should you say?

BUILDING A DUMMY ENGINE

One day last summer Ralph had been thinking what fun it would be to rig up a dummy engine and sit in the cab and play engineer. His thought led him from the back yard into the woodshed.

[Telling a story]

4. In telling the class about your own vacation experience, choose as a subject some one thing that you think will be of interest; then plan your talk carefully so that every one will get a clear idea of just what happened.

5. In order to help the class enjoy your story as you tell it, keep in mind the following directions:

Being Courteous to an Audience

Stand erect before your class in an easy, quiet position. Use a pleasant low voice, but speak so that every one can hear you. Pronounce your words distinctly.

Make your talk interesting and give it without hesitation.

6. As you listen to what others have to say, do what you can to encourage them. Sit quietly, keep your eyes on the speaker, and thus show that you are ready to enjoy his talk.

[Judging a story]

7. After a number of stories have been told, think them over and be ready to answer these questions: Which contained ideas that you would like to try? Which talks were interesting because they formed a connected story about one thing?

2. A New Accomplishment

I

[Conversation]

1. A vacation is often a time for acquiring new accomplishments as well as for carrying out inter-

esting plans. Perhaps this last summer you have learned to do one of the following things:

To swim   To build a fire
To dive   To mow a lawn
To row a boat   To cook
To ride a bicycle   To sew, knit, or crochet
To play tennis   To run a typewriter
To play basket ball   To use a sewing machine
To signal with flags   To give first aid to the injured
To use a radio set   To drive a horse

2. What new thing have you learned to do that is not mentioned in the list?

3. Robert, one of the boys in this picture, could swim well, but he was afraid to dive. One day last summer he and some of his playmates made a raft out of some old boards and tried to dive from it. When the boys first climbed upon the raft, it tipped them over, and they all fell into the water with a

big splash.   This tumble was such fun and the boys came to the surface so quickly that every one forgot to be frightened.   Soon all of the boys, including Robert, were diving from the raft and doing it well.

[Giving a talk]

4. In acquiring your new accomplishment, did you, like Robert, have any difficulty to overcome?   Did you grow discouraged?   How did you feel when you had really learned what you started out to do?   Be ready to give a talk telling just what happened.

5. After listening to the talks by others, tell from which you received helpful suggestions.   Ask questions about the points that you did not understand.

II

[Judging a talk]

6. Compare the following stories.   Which gives enough facts to make the point clear?

> Last summer my father taught me how to swim.   I went into the water every day.   After a time I learned to swim without help.

> When I first went to camp last summer I could not swim a stroke, and I am ashamed to admit that I was even afraid to go into the water.   One day the camp director gave me a lesson in swimming.   As he held me up in the water, he taught me first how to use my legs and then how to hold my hands and use my arms.   In the next lesson I thought he was holding me, but he was not.   After I had swum around for some time, I looked up.   To my surprise, I saw the director at least five yards away.   He stood smiling at me.

7. Find what is wrong with the following story:

When in the country last summer I learned to drive a team of horses. My father took us to the country in July. My mother went, too, and all of the family. We visited my grandmother who keeps chickens. She has one little bantam. We came home in August. My uncle taught me how to drive. He showed me how to hold the reins and how to pull them when I wished the horses to turn. One horse was lazy. My uncle showed me how to make him do his share of the work.

8. Think over the talks given by the class. Tell which speakers have learned to follow these directions:

Select one point or event as a subject.
Give enough facts to make the story clear.
Keep to the point. Do not tell unnecessary facts.

3. Using Words Correctly

I

Pull up the language weeds.

Make room for the plants to grow

1. Incorrect words, like weeds in a garden, cause trouble. They take the place of correct words and prevent the growth of good habits of speech.

2. To make sure that you are not cultivating some

of the worst weeds in your language garden, look through the following list.   Remember to say:

1. **I saw it** (not *I seen it,* or *I see it yesterday*).[1]
2. **I did the work** (not *I done the work*).[1]
3. **John came early** (not *John come early*).[1]
4. **Mary ran home** (not *Mary run home*).
5. **Dick and I are going** (not *I and Dick are going*).[1]
6. **Tom left** (not *Tom he left*).[1]
7. **He and I play together** (not *Him and me play together*).[1]
8. **It was he who broke the window** (not *It was him who broke the window*).[1]
9. **I haven't a book** (not *I haven't got* or *I hain't got a book*).[1]
10. **I haven't any** or **I have none** (not *I haven't none*).[1]

3. In the list of errors given in parentheses there are two new ones for the boys and girls in the fifth grade to add to those that they are conquering completely.   These are numbers 4 and 8.

Note. The list takes for granted that you never use words like *ain't, youse, yourn, her'n, his'n, hisself, busted,* nor such expressions as *them things, this here, that there, I hain't got no pencil.*   These errors are some of the worst "weeds" that can be allowed to grow.   The sooner they are "pulled up" the better.   The list also takes for granted that you do not use *says* for *said* or *give* instead of *gave.*   It is correct to say, (1) *My father says that I may go* or *My father said I might go* and (2) *My brother gives me presents* or *My brother gave me a present yesterday.*

4. If you make any of the errors named in Exercise 2, you should guard your speech against them at all times.   Perhaps, if you copy the correct expressions and take the list home with you as a reminder, it will help you in forming the right habits.

5. Whenever you try to be of assistance to some one else, keep the following directions in mind:

[1] Allotted to previous grades for the pupils themselves to correct whenever the error is made.

Making a Correction

In making a correction, remember to give the right form. If a classmate named John should say, "My brother and me went home," you might say, "John should have said *my brother and I* in place of *my brother and me*," or you might ask, "John, shouldn't you say *my brother and I* in place of *my brother and me?*" Try to express yourself in a helpful and courteous manner. Do not seem to be finding fault.

II

6. Notice that the sentences in each of the following exercises "match" each other in that they both show the correct use of the words printed in italics. Think of other sentences that match those given.

1. As I *came* to school, I *saw* a flock of birds flying overhead.
   As I *came* to school, I *saw* a truck loaded with barrels.
2. When John was late, he *did* his work hastily.
   When John was early, he *did* his work carefully.
3. When the dog *saw* the rabbit, he *ran* after it.
   When the man *saw* the bear, he *ran* away from it.
4. When my uncle buys a new automobile, *he and I* are going for a drive.
   When my brother buys a box of candy, *he and I* are going to divide it.
5. Mary knew that *it was she* who had broken the window.
   Ruth knew that *it was she* who had lost the doll.
6. Henry has a pencil, but he *hasn't* any paper.
   Mary has a reader, but she *hasn't* an arithmetic.
7. Bats have wings, but they *have no* feathers.
   Moles have ears, but they *have no* eyes.

7. Be ready from day to day, whenever you have

a few minutes to spare, to play the following game:

GAME: *Matching Sentences*

The leader stands before the class and reads a sentence from each section in Exercise 6 in turn, and calls upon different players to give sentences of their own to match those read. If the leader reads, "As I came to school, I saw a flock of birds flying overhead," the player called upon may say, "As I came to school, I saw clouds in the sky."

If a player makes a mistake, the leader gives him the correct form. If the leader fails to notice a mistake, a new leader is chosen.

8. Write sentences that "match" those given in Exercise 6.

4. A Story-Telling Game

I

[Talking in separate sentences]

1. In this story-telling game, each player called upon must tell a story entertainingly and at the same time remember to talk in separate sentences. If he uses the words *and*, *then*, and *so*, except in places where they are needed, he is "caught."

2. Play the game, using this story:

LITTLE JACK SPARROW

Little Jack Sparrow was a tattletale. Whenever he had any news, he told it to the first person he met.

One day Jack Sparrow met Mr. Wolf. He called, "Oh, Mr. Wolf! I have something to tell you!"

The wolf pretended not to hear. Jack Sparrow flew nearer. This time he shouted in a loud voice, "Oh, Mr. Wolf! I have something to tell you!"

"I am deaf in one ear and can't hear out of the other," answered Mr. Wolf. "Come a little nearer."

Little Jack Sparrow flew nearer. He lit on Mr. Wolf's nose. Mr. Wolf opened his mouth, — and nothing more was ever seen of Little Jack Sparrow, the tattletale.

[Using other words in place of *and*]

3. **Which of these sentences sounds better?**

There was once a tattletale *and he* was called Jack Sparrow.

There was once a tattletale *who* was called Jack Sparrow.

And is sometimes a troublesome word. To avoid having difficulty with **it**, try to leave it out when it is unnecessary and to use instead *who, which*, and *that* to connect your thoughts.

4. Complete:

Jack Sparrow met Mr. Wolf, ——— pretended that he was hard of hearing.

5. Play the game, using these fables; but this time you may either repeat one of the fables given or you may make up one of your own.

THE QUARREL

Two little chickens that were searching for food came upon a stalk of fine plump wheat. Instead of dividing it evenly, they began to fight over it. They struck at each other first with their claws and then with their beaks until they were quite worn out. While they were fighting thus, a crow, flying overhead, caught a glimpse of the stalk of wheat and saw the chickens quarreling. He thought to himself, "This is a fine chance to get a dinner for myself." Thereupon he seized the wheat and carried it off.

A CRAFTY FOX

A farmer one night discovered a fox in his poultry house, killing his chickens. Seizing a heavy stick, the farmer struck him a blow on the head, and the fox fell over, apparently dead. The man threw the fox over his shoulder. As he carried him toward his house, he began thinking of what a fine rug he would make from the fox's skin.

But the fox was not dead. As the farmer approached his house, the fox decided that it was time for action; whereupon he bit the man in the leg. In surprise and pain the farmer loosened his hold, and the fox scampered off toward the woods.

[Telling original fables]

6. Instead of the first story you may tell, if you wish (1) about two sparrows fighting over a crust of bread, (2) about two dogs fighting over a bone, or (3) about two boys quarreling over a piece of cake. For the second story you may tell (1) about a hunter capturing a tiger, (2) about a bear playing "'possum," or (3) about a boy meeting a snake. What other subjects can you suggest?

II

[Practice in using other words in place of *and*]

7. Give sentences that "match" the following:

The fox had been stealing chickens *which* belonged to a farmer.

8. Complete, using *who*, *which*, or *that* to connect a new thought with the one given:

1. The fox was discovered by a farmer ———.
2. The farmer struck the fox ———.
3. The chickens did not see the crow ———.
4. The crow ate the wheat ———.

9. Besides *who*, *which*, and *that*, the words *but*, *when*, *where*, and *if* are often used to join the parts of a sentence.

Complete:

1. The farmer thought the fox was dead, but ———
2. The fox ran to the woods when ———
3. Little Jack Sparrow lit on Mr. Wolf's nose, where ———
4. Little Jack Sparrow would not have met danger if ———

10. If you had trouble in telling the stories, you are to try again. Get some one to listen to you and afterwards to answer these questions: Was the story told entertainingly? Was it told in separate sentences without unnecessary *and*'s, *so*'s, and *then*'s?

[Written exercise]

11. Complete Exercises 8 and 9 in writing. In order to have your paper neat in appearance, try to follow the directions given on page 290.

5. A Foolish Scare

I

[Conversation]

1. Most scares prove to be foolish ones, which we laugh about afterwards. Have you ever been frightened in the dark or elsewhere at a queer sound? Have you ever been frightened by a dog or a cat? Tell when it happened.

2. Find out what frightened the boy who told the following story.

ALONE IN THE DARK

One evening I was badly frightened.   My father left me alone in a car while he went into a farmhouse on business.   As I sat waiting in the dark, I heard a slight noise in the distance.   The sound was that of an animal coming steadily toward me.   The soft footfalls kept coming nearer and nearer until they were at the side of the car.   Trembling with fear, I looked up expecting to see a wild animal leap into sight.   To my surprise I found standing near the car a large shepherd dog ready to make friends with me.

[Choosing a good beginning for a story]

3. How does the first sentence in the story in Exercise 2 help to interest you in what the boy has to say?

4. Read the following sentences; then give at least one other sentence that would make a good beginning for a story:

a. One evening when I was in the cellar, I heard a strange noise.

b. I shall never forget the first time I was left alone in the house.

c. I had a queer experience last Hallowe'en.

d. I used to be afraid of the dark.

e. Near the place where we spend our summers, we often see snakes.

5. Your class will be interested in hearing about some scare that you have had.   Choose a good beginning and then take a few minutes to think how you can tell the story so that every one will understand how frightened you were.

6. Before telling your story, give the beginning that you have chosen.   Let those in the class decide

whether or not they would like to hear the rest of the story.

II

[Review. The use of capitals]

7. Can you write a story like this one and use capital letters where they are needed? Think of the rule for each capital:

A Cat in the Cellar

After supper yesterday Mother sent me to the cellar for coal. As I was carrying the coal up the stairs, I heard a scratching sound. I was so frightened that I dropped the coal and ran up the stairs shouting, "Mother! Mother! There is some one in the cellar!"

Mother laughed and said, "Oh, Fred! It is only the cat."

8. Find in Exercise 7 an illustration for each of these rules:

Begin with a capital

The first word of a sentence.
All words used as proper names.
All important words in the title of a story.

Note. In writing titles, begin each of the following words with a small letter except when using it at the beginning:
a, an, the, of, for, to, in, and

The first word of a group of words spoken by some one.

Write the word *I* as a capital.

[Written exercise]

9. To make sure that you understand the rules, copy them and write an example after each; or, if you prefer, you may show their use in a story of your own like the one in Exercise 7.

6. In Mischief

I

One

Two

Three

Four

[Conversation]

1. Gordon was an active baby who was so intent on finding out about the world that he often got

into trouble. One day some one left a globe of goldfish on the floor. Of course Gordon was interested in the shining fish that were darting to and fro, so he decided to go fishing. You can tell from the pictures what happened. What do you imagine made Gordon cry? What do you suppose Gordon's mother said to him when she rescued the goldfish?

2. What mischief do you remember getting into when you were little? What mischief have you seen a baby doing?

3. It is not always *little* children who get into mischief. Sometimes, as this story shows, older children find themselves in trouble.

MY REPORT CARD

I have reason to remember what happened the time that I took my report card home with my deportment marked *poor*. I hid my card under my sweater and walked home with lagging footsteps. I sat down to lunch hoping Mother would forget to ask for the card, but I had no such luck. When lunch was nearly over, she asked, "Isn't this the day for your report card?" When I did not answer promptly, she said, "Let me see it at once!"

I will leave you to guess what happened next. I can say only this: I have been careful ever since never to get *poor* in my deportment.

[Choosing a good ending for a story]

4. What thought ends the story in Exercise 3 so that you know that nothing more will be said? Why did the boy who told the story leave you to guess what happened after he showed his report card?

5. In telling the story of the baby and the goldfish, (see Exercise 1) what ending could you use to show that the baby will never touch the goldfish again?

6. Think how you might end a story of a naughty child running away from home; of a boy helping himself to forbidden jam; of a puppy that thought his master's best shoes were meant for playthings.

7. With the help of one of the following sugges- tions, plan a story to tell your class:

a. Tell a story about the picture, using this begin- ning or one of your own:

One day Gordon's mother left him alone in a room where a globe of goldfish stood on the floor.

b. Tell a story of your own about getting into mischief.

In planning a story, remember to keep to one point, to tell enough facts to make the story interesting, and to choose a good beginning and ending.

II

[Review. Punctuation]

8. Point out the marks of punctuation and tell for what purpose each is used.

I walked home with lagging footsteps.
Mother asked, "Isn't this the day for your report card?"
Mother said, "Let me see it at once!"

9. Study the sentences in Exercise 8; then close your book and write them.   If you make an error, you are to try again.

[Written exercise]

10. Copy these rules, writing an example after each:

Place a period at the end of each sentence that is a statement.

Place a question mark at the end of each question.

Place an exclamation point after a word or sentence that is an exclamation.

Use quotation marks to enclose in a sentence the exact words spoken by some one.

Use one or more commas to set off from the rest of the sentence the words that are quoted.

7. Review and Summary

I. The Meaning and Pronunciation of Words

1. In the lessons in this chapter you have used the words printed in italics. Pronounce each one distinctly; then show its meaning by using it in a sentence of your own:

1. Fairy stories are *entertaining*.
2. Diving is a new *accomplishment* for me.
3. In making *suggestions* to our classmates, we try to be courteous.
4. The dog was *frightened* when he saw a bear.
5. The boy walked with *lagging* footsteps when he was sent to his father to be punished.

2. The following words are often mispronounced. Make sure that you can pronounce each correctly:

get	hundred	something	which
just	children	nothing	when
can	asked	going	why
catch	across	writing	what
throw	wished	reading	where
old	because	laughing	while

II. The Use of Capitals and Marks of Punctuation

3. Think of a reason for each capital and mark of punctuation; then after studying the selection, practice writing it with your book closed until you can write it correctly:

From a Fairy Tale

"Alas!" said the prince. "What shall I do? I have not yet found a dog small enough."

"Never fear," said the White Cat. "I will see that you have a dog."

III. The Sentence and the Paragraph

4. Show that you know the meaning of the following definitions by finding in the stories on pages 9 and 10 several examples of each:

A sentence expresses a complete thought.
A paragraph consists of one or more sentences on one topic.

5. Write a paragraph made up of the sentences that answer the following questions. First think of a title.

What game do you like to play best? How many players does it take? Where do you play it? What do you do first? What do you do after that? How do you know who wins?

6. Choose a beginning of your own or one of these beginnings and write a paragraph. Remember to write in separate sentences and to keep to one point.

Saturday I had a good time playing ———.
My little brother is mischievous.
The other day I had a surprise.
Last week I made ———.
I am learning to ———.

7. If your work in Exercise 6 is not satisfactory, you should ask for help and then try the exercise again.

8. Using Words Correctly

Test A.   First Form.   Ten Common Errors

Copy and complete the statements, filling the blanks with words from the list given below Number 4:

1. We ——— birds flying south.
2. The flock ——— from the north.
3. The boys ——— their work well.
4. The children ——— home.

saw	come	done	ran
seen	came	did	run

Copy and complete the answers, using words that make sense:

5. Why isn't Ruth studying?   She ——— no book.
6. Have you her book?   No, I ——— it.

Copy the answers, filling blanks with the words given below Number 10:

7. Where did you and your cousin go?   My cousin and ——— went to a ball game.
8. Where did you and your sister go?   ——— and ——— went to a play.
9. Where did you and your father go?   ——— and ——— went for a drive.
10. Is it Fred who has my book?   No, it isn't ———.

me	I	she	her	he	him

If your record in Test A is not perfect, you should use the Practice Exercises beginning on page 263.

Chapter II — SCHOOL NEWS

1. Planning a Class Diary

[Conversation]

Have you ever thought what fun it would be to keep a record of what your class does? Each month papers could be written telling of interesting events. The best of these could be selected and bound together in a little book. That would give you a chance to recall all the fine things accomplished by your class, to laugh again at jokes, and to enjoy once more the best stories told. At the end of the year you could give the book with pictures of your class to your teacher, as a keepsake. Wouldn't that be an interesting thing to do, and wouldn't your teacher like to have such a keepsake?

In planning such a class record, or diary, try to decide first of all the kind of stories to include. You will, of course, wish to have in the book stories of anything remarkable done by the members of the class outside of school as well as in school and on the playground. Think what would be interesting.

2. Writing for the Class Diary

I

[Conversation]

1. For one of the first papers to be bound in your class diary, perhaps some one would like to write a description of your class. If this is so, will you try to help him with the information called for in these questions?

> How many boys are there in the class? How many girls are there? How many new members belong to the class? How many of you have been together since you started in school in the kindergarten or in the first grade? Is the class lively and full of fun and at the same time industrious and helpful? In which school subject do most of you do the best work? In what ways are you trying to improve yourselves?

2. Other members of the class may write news items or describe school scenes. Has your class done anything unusually interesting in drawing, in music, in geography, or in any other subject? Have you been on a nature walk or an excursion? Has the baseball team played any games? Have you had an unusually successful fire drill? Has anything funny happened?

3. Be ready to tell a story that you think could be used in the class diary. After giving it, ask the members of the class for their opinions and for suggestions.

[Written composition]

4. Be sure that your talk forms a single connected story, and then write it so that it will be ready for use. Keep in mind the directions printed on page 290.

II

[Finding sentence endings]

5. Look through these stories to find where periods belong; then read them with other members of the class, each in turn giving a sentence.

THE DIRIGIBLE

Yesterday at school we heard a great buzzing overhead we looked out and saw a great airship, or dirigible, flying near it looked like a big sausage we all went to the windows and watched it as it rose slowly, crossed the river, and disappeared from sight.

A MAIL ORDER

To help in our study of birds, our class ordered some pictures from the Perry Picture Company we wrote a letter, made out a money order slip, and then got a money order from the post office to-day the pictures arrived and we all felt proud that we had done the ordering ourselves.

A FIRE DRILL

Clang! Clang! goes the bell pencils drop to the floor books are hastily closed without stopping for coats, we form our lines and, followed by our teacher, we march through the corridor, down one side of the steps, and out into the yard in a minute the building is empty.

[Proof-reading]

6. Read your story (see Exercise 4) to make sure that you have placed a period at the end of each sentence.

7. Look through your paper again to make sure that it contains no errors in spelling or in the use of capitals.

[Judging papers]

8. After your class has handed all of the papers to your teacher, perhaps she will read a number of the best and let you decide which you would like to keep as a part of the class diary.

9. If you have trouble in writing in separate sentences, you may copy two or more of the stories given in Exercise 5.   First make sure that you know where each sentence ends.

3. Help in the Spelling of Words

1. On page 301 is a list of words to help you in writing words that are often misspelled.   Look at the initial letters of the words and then tell in what order the words are arranged.

2. If you had any one of the following words in mind, under what letter should you look for it?

always   doctor   business   enough   often

3. Why does the word *forty* occur in the dictionary before *friend*?   Why does *making* occur before *many*?

4. Tell in what order the words in each of the following groups occur in a dictionary.

1. attempt	3. Christmas	5. family	7. judge
afraid	celebration	fair	January
always	captain	factory	justice

2. bridge	4. dozen	6. fourth	8. nearly
believe	doctor	forty	neither
beautiful	doubt	forenoon	navy

5. Turn to page 301.   See how quickly you can

find the different words that your teacher calls for. Be ready to spell them.

6. Write the words in Exercise 4 in the order in which they occur in the dictionary.

4. Sending News to Friends

[Writing thoughtful letters]

1. With the news items in mind that you planned for your diary, think of some one who would be particularly glad to hear from your class. Choose a member who has moved out of town or some one who is absent, and plan a letter to him.

2. The following letter was written by a big boy to a little girl. What did he choose to say that would interest her?

Portland, Maine
March 10, 1927

Dear Harriet,

I am very sorry to hear that you are sick. I do hope that you will be better soon and come to school again.

Since you have been away, we have bought three bird houses. The two large ones we put on poles, but the little one we placed in a tree. I wonder what kind of bird will visit our little houses first. I should like to have a bluebird come, but I suppose you would choose to have bold Robin Redbreast for the first visitor, wouldn't you?

Sincerely your friend,
Herbert Richmond

3. Without re-reading the letter, tell what the first paragraph is about. What is the second paragraph about?

4. Notice that this rule was followed in writing the letter:

Begin a new paragraph with each new topic.

5. Before writing your letter, decide what news would interest the person to whom you are writing; then think of a good opening sentence.

6. As your teacher writes on the board for you, dictate the letter to her.

7. Study the rules on page 294; then do one of the following things:

a. Make a neat copy of the letter written on the board.
b. Write a letter of your own to be sent with the class letter.
c. Think of a teacher who would be glad to hear from you.   Write a letter telling her what you remember best about the time when you were in her class.

8. What care will you take in paragraphing your letter?

5. For the Story Hour. Funny Stories, Riddles, and Conundrums

I

[Leading up to a surprise]

1. Most funny stories contain a surprise. Something unexpected happens, or something unusual is said.

2. Find the surprise in each of these stories.

THE LITTLE STUDENT

"Mother," said little Bessie, who was just learning to make figures, "can you make 'thirteen'?"

"Certainly, my dear," answered the mother.

"Then I wish you'd show me how," continued the little student. "I can make the 'thirt' all right, but I can't make the 'teen.'"

A SUM IN ARITHMETIC

Little Neal was sitting at the breakfast table when his mother asked him how many pancakes he had eaten.

"Three," he answered.

"If you ate three more, how many would that make?" questioned his mother.

"Well," replied Neal slowly, "I guess it would make a tummy-full."

MERELY A MAN

Little Irene ran into the room breathlessly.

"Oh, Mother!" she said, "don't scold me for being late for supper, because I've had such a disappointment. A horse fell down and they said they were going to send for a horse doctor, so I waited and waited, and what do you think? It wasn't a horse doctor at all. It was only a man.

FOOD FOR THE BIRD

Johnny, aged four, went into a grocery and asked for a box of canary seed.

"Is it for your mother?" asked the grocer.

"No, of course not," replied the little fellow. "It's for the bird."

HEARD AT SCHOOL

A teacher in a first grade, who was conducting a reading lesson, wrote 28 on the board, and then said, "This is the page of the reading lesson. What is it, Mary?"

"Eighty-two," announced Mary.

"No, put it the other way round," suggested the teacher.

"Tooty-eight," was Mary's response.

3. Notice that the conversation in the stories on page 26 helps to make them interesting. What words are used to prevent an unpleasant repetition of the word *said?* Make a list of them.

II

[Riddles and conundrums]

4. Can you, with the help of these pictures, guess the riddles given below them?

RIDDLES

Higher than a house;
Higher than a tree!
Oh, whatever can it be?

A riddle, a riddle, I suppose.
A hundred eyes but never a nose.

What shoemaker makes shoes without leather,
With all the four elements put together,
Fire and water, earth and air?
Every customer takes two pair.

5. Here are three conundrums and their answers. What others like them do you know?

CONUNDRUMS

What is the difference between an engineer and a teacher?

Answer.   An engineer minds a train; a teacher trains the mind.

If a barrel weighs ten pounds when empty, what can you fill it with to make it weigh seven pounds?

Answer.   Holes.

What is it you can keep after giving it to another?

Answer.   A promise.

III

[Planning a story hour]

6. Plan a story hour for which every one comes prepared to give a riddle or a conundrum, or to tell a funny story.   Choose a, b, or c.

> a. Give a riddle or a conundrum like one of those given above or on page 27.
> b. Tell one of the funny stories given in Exercise I.
> c. Tell a story new to the class about the bright saying of a little child, or tell one about a queer mistake.

In telling a story, try to lead up to the surprise that it contains and thus make the point of the story clear.

IV

[Writing a conversation in paragraphs]

7. Stories like those on page 26 are printed so that you can easily tell who is speaking.   In the story *Heard at School* two persons speak.   In the first paragraph the teacher is speaking.   Who is reported as speaking in the second paragraph?   In the third?   In the fourth and last?

In writing a conversation, begin a new paragraph with each change of speaker.

[Written composition]

8. Make a neat copy of one of the stories on page 26, and then write a funny story that could be used in the class diary.

6. Review and Summary

I. Pronunciation and Meaning of Words

1. First pronounce each word in italics; then show its meaning by using it in a sentence of your own:

1. The boy when traveling kept a *diary*.
2. The story was a *paragraph* long.
3. The letter was neat in *appearance*.
4. History was the *favorite* study of the class.
5. Some of the boys and girls liked *geography* better.

2. In the excitement of playing games, boys and girls sometimes run their words together. Show how each of the following expressions should be said, and then be on your guard against slighting any of the words:

Let me go.	I don't know.
Let them go.	Look at them.
Give me the ball.	Come here.
What did you say?	Where are you going?
Won't you go?	Do you have to go?

II. Using Words Meaning More than One

3. Tell which of the following words means one and which means more than one:

letter   letters

When a word means one person, place, or thing, it is *singular* in number.

When a word means more than one, it is *plural*.

4. Which of these words are plural?   Make a list
of them.

boy	boys	knife	knives	fly	flies
toy	toys	life	lives	sky	skies
box	boxes	self	selves	berry	berries
fox	foxes	elf	elves	cherry	cherries

5. Which words in the list above form their plural
by adding *s* to the singular?   Write five others.

6. Write three words not given in the list that
form their plural by adding *es* to the singular; three
that change the *f* to *v* and add *es;* and three that
change the *y* to *i* and add *es.*

7. Using Words Correctly

Test B.   First Form.   Giving Words their Right Meaning

With the help of the words below the test complete each remark made.   Copy only what is said;
not who says it.

1. Mother (to boy): —— your book to school with
you.
2. Teacher (to Alice): You have done your work ——.
3. Conductor: Stand back, please.   —— the passengers out.
4. Man (to his dog): —— down, Tiger.   ——
down, I say.
5. Girl (asking permission of her mother): —— I go
for a drive?
6. Boy (speaking to his teacher): —— I put the
books away?

bring	good	let	lay	can	shall
take	well	leave	lie	may	will

For Practice Exercises see pages 268, 269.

Chapter III — GOOD TIMES READING

1. Old Friends

[Conversation]

1. Many old story-book friends are in this picture. Some of them, like Cinderella, you have known a long time. Which of the others do you recognize?

2. To help your class recall some of the characters in the picture on page 31, be ready to tell in a single clear sentence something about each.

[Making a sentence interesting]

3. Improve the following descriptions by making one sentence of each group. In connecting the ideas, use words like *when* and *which*.

> 1. Hansel and Gretel found a tiny house. The house belonged to a witch.
> 2. Snow White took a bite of the poisoned apple. She fell in a swoon.
> 3. In a deep pool of water the princess lost her golden ball. The ball was found by a frog.

4. Think of some story-book character not shown in the picture. Try to tell in a single interesting sentence something about the character. Remember that:

Every sentence should be clear in meaning and sound well.

5. Be ready to play this game:

SENTENCE GAME: *The House that Jack Built*

> One player starts the game by giving a short sentence about a story-book character. Other players, as shown in the following dialogue, try to make the sentence more interesting by adding other facts:
>
> *First player*. Robin Hood was a bold outlaw.
> *Second player*. Robin Hood was a bold outlaw who lived in the woods.
> *Third player*. Robin Hood was a bold outlaw who lived in the woods with a band of merry men.

In introducing a new thought in a sentence, the players will find these words useful: *when*, *who*, *which*, *that*, *but*, *because*, *if*, *where*, *although*, and *so that*. They should use the word *and* only in those places where they are sure that it is correct.

6. In playing the game the first time, you may use these sentences if you wish:

1. *First player*. Cinderella sat by the fire.
Second player. Cinderella sat by the fire weeping because she could not go to the ball.
Third player. When ———.
2. Robinson Crusoe was shipwrecked.
3. Pinocchio was a jointed wooden boy.
4. Hiawatha lived in a wigwam.
5. Snow White lived with seven dwarfs.
6. The Dutch twins were full of mischief.

2. New Friends

I

[Conversation — Making plans]

1. In order to make new friends among books, your class will enjoy planning three book exhibits. Decide what books you will need in connection with the lessons on pages 35 and 36; then with your teacher's help appoint three committees. Ask one committee to bring to class at least five good books of animal stories; ask another committee to bring interesting stories about boys and girls; and ask the third committee to take charge of the larger exhibition to which you invite another class.

2. The members of the class who have libraries will, perhaps, be willing to lend books. Other members can help in the work by looking up the facts called for in the following outlines.

How to Get Books from a Public Library

Where the nearest public library is situated
How a card for taking out books can be obtained from
the library
How the card is used

Magazines for Boys and Girls

The title of a good magazine
What the magazine contains
Why the magazine is a good one

II

[Writing titles of books]

3. Before copying the lists for your exhibition
and for your own reading, make sure that you can
write the titles of books correctly.

4. Give the reason for the capitals in each of the
following titles (see the rule in Exercise 8 on page 13).

Stories of Great Americans for Little Americans
The King of the Golden River
A Child's Garden of Verses
Alice in Wonderland
In the Days of the Giants

5. Study the titles in Exercise 4; then practice
writing them with your book closed until you can
do so correctly.

6. Read the titles of the books given in Exercise
4, page 36, and Exercise 8, page 37. Notice the
capitals; then make a list of the books to take home
with you. Perhaps you will be able to bring some
of the books to school.

3. Planning a Book Report

I. Animal Tales

[Conversation]

1. In many animal stories, as you know, the small animal gets the better of the large one. The fox outwits the wolf, and the turtle wins a race with the hare. In which stories that you have read does the rabbit come out ahead of his enemies?

2. In a book called *Nights with Uncle Remus* an old colored man tells stories about Brer Rabbit (Brother Rabbit). Look at the picture; then tell, if you can, what animals were always lying in wait for Brer Rabbit. What do you think makes the stories full of fun?

3. The stories about Doctor Dolittle are also funny ones. These tell of exciting adventures of an old doctor and his animal friends. If you have read any of the adventures, you may tell the class which you enjoyed most. Was it the fight with the pirates,

the capture of the pushmi-pullyu (push-me-pull-you),
or was it something else?

4. Tell which of the books in this list you know
and then name others about animals:

Æsop's Fables	Doctor Dolittle's Post-Office
Black Beauty	Jataka Tales
A Book of Fairy-Tale Bears	Just So Stories
Burgess Bedtime Stories	Merry Animal Tales
Cat Stories by Helen	The Pet Book
Hunt Jackson	The Story of Doctor Dolittle
A Dog of Flanders	Wild Animals I Have Known
Doctor Dolittle's Circus	Wild Brother

II. Stories about Boys and Girls

[Conversation]

5. Among the stories about boys and girls *Heidi* is
usually a favorite. If you have never read it, you
are to guess from this picture what it is about.

6. Try to tell, also, what work the children had to do and what fun they may have had on the mountain side.

7. After you have expressed your ideas, ask some one who has read the story to tell you whether you guessed right or not. Ask him also to give the names of the two children in the story and what he thinks is the most interesting thing that happened in the book.

8. Some of the other favorite stories about boys and girls are *The Dutch Twins*, *The Japanese Twins*, the other "*Twin*" books, *The Birds' Christmas Carol*, *Alice in Wonderland*, *Understood Betsey*, and *Arlo*. Can you name still others?

III. Planning Talks

9. Look through the book exhibit of animal stories arranged by one of your committees and the exhibit of books about boys and girls arranged by another. Be ready in your next lesson to recommend one of the books shown or some other good story.

10. Since you will not have time to tell the story, you must decide what you can include in a talk a few sentences long. First express your opinion and ask for that of other members of your class, and then talk over the following suggestions:

a. Give the name of the book. Tell in a sentence or two what the book is about. Give the reasons why you like the book.

b. After naming the book and explaining what it is about, tell what you consider the most interesting part.

c. Hold a book before the class and give its title; describe your favorite among the pictures in the book and tell what it shows about the kind of stories the book contains; then let the class see the picture.

11. To arouse interest in your talk, try to make the opening sentence attractive. Avoid, if you can, using for this purpose a sentence which others in your class have used so often that it has become tiresome. Here are six different beginnings from which you may choose. Perhaps you can think of still others.

1. The best story about boys and girls that I know is ———

2. I have been reading ———. What I like best about it is ———

3. I think you will all enjoy reading ———

4. My favorite story is ———

5. Can you guess the name of this book?

6. Did you ever read ———?

4. Making a Report

I

[Giving talks]

1. Before giving the talk planned in your last lesson, rehearse it to yourself. Make sure that you have chosen something that will interest the class, and that you have expressed your ideas in separate sentences that are clear in meaning and sound well.

2. When you give your talk, try to have on hand the book that you are describing. Show it to the class.

3. After listening to the talks by others, be ready to express your appreciation of the work of the committees and of the boys and girls who have done the most to attract your attention to interesting books. Give them a rising vote of thanks. Some one may say, "I move that we give a rising vote of thanks to Henry, John, and Mary for the work that they have done." Some one else may say, "I second the motion." The one in charge of the class may then say, "All those in favor of the motion will please stand." After the class has voted in this way, the leader may say, "Please be seated. The motion was passed."

4. Later, after you have read a story recommended by some one, you are to tell why you liked the story.

II

5. When the title of a book or story is written in a sentence it must in some way be set off from the rest of the sentence. Find in the following statements the titles of stories and tell how they are printed:

Wild Brother is a story of a bear cub brought up with a family of children.

The story of Redruff is found in *Wild Animals I Have Known*.

The Jataka Tales are stories of crocodiles, monkeys, and other animals found in India.

6. Words that are printed in italics are underlined in writing; therefore, we should keep in mind the following rule.

Underline all titles of books and stories when they are used in sentences.

7. Give the reason for each capital in Exercise 5.

8. Study the sentences in Exercise 5 and then write them with your book closed. How will you make sure that your paper is correct?

9. Write five or more other sentences containing the names of books or stories.

5. Something to Guess

[Making pictures with words]

1. Try to tell in what book each picture belongs:

In a tiny house in the woods a little girl is keeping house for seven dwarfs. She is very beautiful. Her skin is as white as snow, her hair is as black as ebony, and her cheeks are as red as a rose. A wicked queen, dressed as a peddler, is trying to sell her a poisoned apple.

Sauntering across a field, in sight of his enemies, is a little rabbit, dressed like a dandy and looking innocent. Peeping over a hilltop can be seen a fox, a raccoon, a turkey buzzard, and a bear.

It is early afternoon, but the sun is setting, and the snow on a mountain peak is aglow with the color of a rose. Two children are herding goats and watching the color on the snow. Near them are pastures in which flowers are growing. In the distance on the mountains are glaciers, or fields of ice and snow.

2. Compare these descriptions. Tell why the second one is better than the first.

Three small ships are crossing the ocean. In one is a man looking for land.

Three small ships are crossing the ocean. On the deck of the largest ship stands a man with a telescope, searching for land. Near him are sailors who frown and mutter. They are afraid that they will come to the edge of the world and fall off, or be devoured by monsters.

3. Make this description more interesting:

Two rosy children wearing wooden shoes are sitting beside their grandfather.

4. Think out a description, or riddle, of your own like those in Exercise 1 and be ready to give it. Tell enough to make the riddle interesting, but do not give away too quickly what you are describing. Keep the class guessing.

6. A Book Exhibit

[Planning an exhibition]

1. With the help of the committee appointed in the lesson on page 33, plan a book exhibit to which you invite another class. Perhaps you can be of service to the boys and girls in the class by telling them about the books that you have liked best.

2. First talk over the kinds of books that you would like to have in the exhibition and how you can help the committee in charge to get them. You may wish to include animal stories, fairy tales, books about boys and girls, stories from history, song books, books of poetry, and books telling how to do things.

3. After you have collected your books and have talked them over, choose some one to write on the board a short list of books that you would like to

recommend to your visitors.   Leave the list on the board so that neat copies may be made for your guests.

[Planning a program]

4. In planning the program for the entertainment at your exhibition, decide, with your teacher's help, which boys and girls are to do different things.   Choose members of the class:

a. To show their favorite books and tell the visitors about them.
b. To give riddles about books (see page 40).
c. To read or tell stories.
d. To give quotations about books.
e. To pass out book lists for the visitors to carry away with them.

5. If you wish, you may use these quotations as part of your program.   First decide what each one means; then learn one of them.

A book's a magic sort of thing
That makes you sailor, chief, or king.
When I am old and own a shelf,
I think I'll have a book myself!
MARY CAROLYN DAVIES

We may see how all things are —
Seas and cities, near and far,
And the flying fairies' looks,
In the picture story-books.
ROBERT LOUIS STEVENSON

Books are keys to wisdom's treasure;
Books are gates to lands of pleasure;
Books are paths that upward lead;
Books are friends.   Come, let us read.
EMILIE POULSSON

[Writing an invitation]

6. In inviting the guests to your book exhibit, what can you say to make them feel that you really wish them to accept your invitation? Why must you include the time and place of entertainment?

7. As your teacher writes the invitation on the board for you, tell her what to say; then choose some one to copy the note.

7. A Christmas Story

I

[Learning to study]

1. A miser is, as you know, a person who becomes so fond of his money that he cannot bear to spend it. This story of *Wee Red Cap* tells about the strange adventures of a miser at Christmas time.

WEE RED CAP [1]

It was Christmas Eve and Tieg sat alone by his fire with naught in his cupboard but a pinch of tea and a bare mixing of meal. His heart inside him was as soft and warm as the ice on the water bucket outside the door. Tieg was too stingy to help the widow who lived next door to him, or even to share his hearth at Christmas time with his old friend Barney.

As he sat thinking of his gold, Tieg heard a child who was passing, sing:

"*Open the door and greet ye the stranger.*"

At this Tieg put his fingers deep in his ears, saying, "Can't a man live as he wishes without being pestered by a song in this way?"

[1] Adapted from *This Way to Christmas* by Ruth Sawyer. Courtesy of Harper & Brothers.

Then a strange thing happened; hundreds and hundreds of tiny lights began dancing outside the window, making the room bright. Slowly without a creak or a cringe the door opened, and in there trooped a crowd of the Good People, or fairies.

Tieg was filled with wonder when he saw the fairies; but, when they saw him, they laughed.

"We are taking your cabin this night, Tieg," said they. "You are the only man hereabout with an empty hearth, and we are needing one."

Without saying more, the fairies bustled about making the room ready. They spread out a feast and then pipers came. The feasting began and the pipers played, and never had Tieg seen such a sight in his life. Suddenly a wee man sang out:

"Clip, clap, clip, clap. I wish I had my wee red cap," and out of the air there tumbled the neatest cap Tieg had ever laid his two eyes on. The wee man clapped it on his head, crying:

"I wish I were in Spain!" and — whist! — up the chimney he went, and away out of sight.

Then another wee man called for his cap, and away he went after the first. Then another and another went until the room was empty, and Tieg sat alone again.

"I'd like to travel that way myself," said Tieg. "It would be a grand saving of tickets, and you get to a place before you have had time to change your mind. Faith, there will be no harm done if I try it."

So Tieg sang the fairies' rhyme and out of the air dropped a wee cap for him and — whist! — up the chimney he went and found himself in Spain.

He was in a great city. The doorways of the houses were hung with flowers and the air was sweet with their smell. At a church door was a crowd of beggars.

"What is the meaning of this crowd of people?" asked Tieg of one of the fairies who had arrived ahead of him.

"They are waiting for the people to come out of church who, on Christmas eve, give half of what they have to those who have nothing."

Then far down the street came a child's voice singing:

"*Feed ye the hungry and rest ye the weary.*"

"Can a song fly after you?" said Tieg angrily. Then, as he heard the fairies cry, "Holland!" he too cried, "Holland!"

In one leap Tieg was over France and over Belgium and standing by the frozen canals over which skated hundreds of lads and maids. Outside of each door stood a wee wooden shoe empty.

"What is the meaning of these shoes?" Tieg asked a fairy.

"You poor fellow," cried the wee man, "don't you know anything? This is the gift night of the year when every man gives to his neighbor."

And again Tieg heard a voice singing:

"*Open the door and greet ye the stranger.*"

At this Tieg angrily set his red cap firmly on his head saying, "I'm for another country."

I cannot tell you half of the adventures Tieg had

that night, nor half the sights he saw. But he passed by
fields that held sheaves of grain for the birds, and doorsteps that held bowls of porridge for the weé creatures.
He saw lighted trees, sparkling and heavy with gifts;
and he stood outside of churches watching crowds pass
in bearing gifts to the Holy Mother and Child.

At last the fairies straightened their caps and cried,
"Now for the great hall in the King of England's palace!"

Whist! — and away they went and Tieg after them;
and the first thing he knew he was in London in a hall
filled with lords and ladies. The doors were wide open
for the poor to come in and warm themselves by the
King's fire and feast at the King's table.

As Tieg watched the people again he heard the song:

"Feed ye the hungry and rest ye the weary."

Then anger overcame Tieg. "I'll stop your pestering
tongue," said he and catching the cap from his head he
threw it at the singer.

No sooner was the cap gone than every soul in the hall
saw Tieg. The next moment they were about him,
catching at his coat and crying:

"Where is he from? What does he here? Take him
to the King!"

Tieg was dragged before the throne.

"He was stealing," cried one.

"He looks evil!" cried another. "Kill him."

All in a moment the voices took up the words and
the hall rang with "Kill him."

But Tieg, trembling with fear, managed to say to the
King, "I have done no evil."

"Maybe," said the King. "But have you done any
good? Come, tell us, have you given aught to any one
to-night? If you have, we will pardon you."

Not a word could Tieg say.

"Then you must die," said the King. "Have you
any last favor to ask?"

"There is a wee red cap I should like to have that I lost a while ago," said Tieg.

The cap was found and in a minute Tieg had it on his head.

"Clip, clap, clip, clap! I wish I were at home," Tieg hastened to say.

Up over the heads of the crowd Tieg flew, and — whist! he found himself back in his own cabin ready to keep Christmas and to share his gold with his neighbors.

2. Tell one thing in the story that interested you; let your classmates give other facts.[1]

[Telling a story in relays]

3. Be ready to help others tell the story in relays. First think of a title for each section and then study the part that you are asked to give. As you study your section, notice that the conversation in it helps to make the story a lively one.

---

[1] GAME. *Tell One Thing.* In playing this game, each person called upon must tell in a single clear sentence some one thing that happened in the story. The players pay no attention to the order in which the events occur, but each must be careful not to repeat what some one else has given.

II

[Making up a story]

4. You have often heard how Christmas is celebrated in Norway. What do you think Tieg may have seen there? What might have happened if he had visited France or America? After you have chosen a country for Tieg to visit, you may write a story telling of his adventures there.

8. Writing for the Class Diary

[Conversation and oral composition]

1. As you recall what has happened at school lately, decide what would be interesting to report in your class diary. Be ready to give stories that you could use.

[Group story]

2. There is one item you will wish, of course, to have in your class diary. That is an account of your book exhibit. Think over just what you would like to say and then dictate the story to your teacher as she writes on the board. Do not forget to tell, among other things, when and where you held your exhibit and who was invited to it.

[Written composition]

3. After the story is erased from the blackboard, the class is to divide itself into two sections. Those who would like to write the story of the book exhibit are to form one section. Those who prefer to write the stories that they composed in Exercise 1 are to form the other section.

4. Decide where each sentence in the following selection ends. Read the story with the members of your class, each one of you in turn giving a sentence:

GIVING A PLAY

A few days ago some of us boys gave a play which we made up from the story of the King of the Golden River everything went well even the mountain scene the arrangement of which taxed our brains to the utmost there were not many of us taking part so some of us had to act more than one character this predicament caused a good deal of bustle behind the scenes the worst time was when Gluck the hero had to change to the constable and hurry in to arrest the Black Brothers.

5. Read your paper (see Exercise 3) to make sure that you have placed a period at the end of each sentence.

6. Choose a good speller to write on the board all the hard words in the papers written by the class. Ask him to write any word in your paper about which you have any doubt.

7. Proof-read your paper for spelling and then hand it to your teacher. Perhaps she will read a number of the best papers and let you choose the ones you would like to put in the class diary.

9. Making a List of Books to Own

1. The following are lists of books that two fifth grade children thought they would like to own. Could you write such a list and have it correct in every way?

Albert's List	*Alice's List*
Dictionary	Three Years with the Poets
Bird Neighbors	Stories of Great Musicians
Red Indian Stories	Grimm's Fairy Tales
Doctor Dolittle's Circus	The Japanese Twins
True Stories from History	Heidi

2. Think over the books that you know; then make a list of five or six that you would like to own. Put a star after the one that you would like to have first. Perhaps, if you take the list home, some one will give you one of the books on your birthday or at Christmas; or, better still, it may be that your father or mother will tell you of a way in which you can earn money with which to buy the book that you starred. Be sure to choose a good book so that you will never regret your choice.

10. Review and Summary

I. Pronunciation and Meaning of Words

1. First pronounce each word printed in italics and then show its meaning by using it in a sentence of your own:

1. A committee was *appointed* to make a list of books.
2. The class arranged an *exhibition* of books.
3. The class prepared an interesting *program*.
4. The children received an *invitation*.
5. The boys *recommended* their favorite books.

2. The words printed here in italics are over-worked. What ones can be used in place of them?

Heidi was *got* at a bookstore.
It was a *fine* book.

3. Practice pronouncing:

morning	having	library	yesterday
singing	learning	February	handkerchief
working	playing	contrary	garage

II. Contractions

4. In conversation, we often shorten words. We say *don't* for *do not* and *I'm* for *I am.*

Don't and *I'm* are called **contractions.**

5. Study these contractions and the words for which they stand:

haven't	have not	I'll	I will
don't	do not	you'll	you will
doesn't	does not	we're	we are
won't	will not	it's	it is
can't	cannot	o'er	over

6. Find three different contractions in the story of *Wee Red Cap.* Find two in the first quotation on page 42.

7. Tell for what each of these words stands: *couldn't, wouldn't, shouldn't, didn't, you've, they'll, you're, ne'er.*

8. With your book closed, make a list of at least fifteen contractions and the words for which they stand.

9. Copy from page 45 and elsewhere five or more sentences containing contractions.

III. Using an Index

10. The index at the back of this book is arranged

in alphabetical order.   Under what letter should you look for each of the following items?

Sentence, definition of   Correcting errors
Paragraph, definition of   Titles of books in sentences
Letter form   Writing a conversation

11. With the help of the index find the pages on which the items in Exercise 10 occur.   Turn to the pages; study the definitions and directions; then be ready to answer questions that your teacher asks you.

11. Using Words Correctly

Test C. First Form. Telling What Happened

Copy the second statement in each exercise, using a form of the word printed in italics to complete it:

Illustration: The bell *rang*.   The bell had *rung*.

1. The boy *wrote* a letter.   The boy had ——— a letter.

2. The class *had given* an entertainment.   The class ——— an entertainment.

3. The meeting *had begun* at three o'clock.   The meeting ——— at three o'clock.

4. The sailors *threw* the cargo overboard.   The sailors had ——— the cargo overboard.

5. The ship *came* from the north.   The ship had ——— from the north.

6. The man *went* away.   The man had ——— away.

7. The child *broke* a window.   The child had ——— a window.

8. The class *saw* a parade.   The class had ——— a parade.

Those failing to make a perfect record on the test should use the Practice Exercises, pages 270–274.

Chapter IV
STORIES OF DOGS AND OTHER PETS
1. Rival Pets

[Conversation]

1. The three pets shown in the picture are great favorites. If you could choose one of them, which should you take?

2. If you were trying to make some one else think that a cat is the very best kind of pet to have, you might show that:

> A cat likes to be played with and petted.
> It has pretty harmless ways.
> It is easily cared for.
> It is useful.

3. What could you say to show that a cat likes

to be played with and petted?   To prove each of the other points given in Exercise 2?

4. Some people prefer a dog to a cat for a pet. What three or four points could you bring out to show that a dog makes a good pet?   Write them on the board.

5. What can you say in favor of a horse or a pony for a pet?

[Giving reasons for an opinion]

6. Choose the pet that you like best and give a talk that will make others see why you like the pet.   If you wish, you may use one of these beginnings:

    a. My favorite pet is a cat.
    b. A dog makes a good pet.
    c. I should like to own a horse (or a pony).

In giving your talk, try to tell enough facts to make your point clear.

7. After you have listened to the talks, take a vote of the class to see which speaker gave the best reasons for his choice of a pet.

2. Clever Tricks

[Conversation]

1. On page 55 there is a picture of Sam, a dog that can spell his name, do sums in arithmetic, and perform other clever tricks.   Since Sam cannot talk, how can he spell his name?   How without cards can he give the answer when his master asks him for the sum of 2 and 3?

2. Some of the common tricks done by dogs are "begging," "saying prayers," and "playing dead dog." Which of these tricks have you seen? With what other tricks are you familiar?

[Learning to study]

3. A cat as well as a dog may show unusual intelligence, and, like the one in this story, may find a way out of a difficulty.

TABBY'S MOVING DAY

Tabby and her three kittens had a snug home in the hay in the barn. One day she found the best possible place for a nest for her family. It was in a trunk full of old clothes in the attic of the house! She picked up one of the kittens and carried it into the house, where she deposited it in the trunk. Then she went back to fetch another kitten. But, while she was away, the mistress of the house chanced to go to the attic. Seeing that the trunk was open, she closed and locked it. She did not know that there was a kitten in it.

When Tabby returned with the second kitten and found the trunk shut, she was in great distress. She cried so piteously that her mistress thought she was hungry, and got her a saucer of milk.   But Tabby did not want milk; she wanted her kitten.   At length by running toward the attic, and then back toward her mistress, she succeeded in leading her to the trunk.   Then by scratching it, she made the woman understand that she wished to have the trunk opened.

As soon as the lid was raised Tabby leaped into the trunk, seized the kitten, and carried it back to the nest in the barn.   She returned immediately for the second kitten, and carried it home without any waste of time. After this experience she was content to keep her kittens in the barn.

4. Tell one thing that happened in the story; let the class tell others; [1] then think of paragraph topics that would help you in telling the entire story.

5. What clever trick have you seen a cat do? What tricks have you seen a horse do?

[Making a story clear]

6. In telling the class about a pet, choose c or d if possible; otherwise choose a or b:

a. Explain how the dog Sam does his tricks.
b. Tell the story of *Tabby's Moving Day*.
c. Tell about some trick that you have seen a dog, a horse, or a cat do.
d. Tell the story of an experience that you have had in training an animal to do a trick; or tell a story that you have read.

In giving your talk, keep in mind what you have learned: tell a connected story about one thing, give enough facts to make the story clear, and keep to the point.   What care will you take in your use of the sentence?   In your use of words?

[1] See the footnote on page 47.

3. Caring for a Pet

[Conversation]

1. If you have ever cared for a pet of your own, you must have learned many facts that would be helpful to other boys and girls who have pets. Be ready to tell what some of them are.

2. These directions show you how to take care of a dog. What new ideas do you gain from them?

TAKING CARE OF A DOG

You should feed a dog two meals a day. Give him one meal before breakfast and the other about four or five o'clock in the afternoon. If you can, give him cooked meat or bread soaked in gravy, some plain vegetables, and mush, all mixed together, and once in a while, give him a bone to gnaw upon.

For a sleeping place, a big dog should have an outdoor kennel that is dry and clean. Smaller dogs may sleep on a piece of carpet in the corner of a hall or an empty bedroom, but not in a cellar. Very small dogs and those that are not strong should have soft beds. A delicate dog should have a basket or a box of the right size, with a cushion or a blanket in it.

Adapted from Olive Thorne Miller.

3. Which of the facts called for in these outlines can you give?

TAKING CARE OF A CAT WITH KITTENS

I. The care of the mother cat: the food and drink that should be given her; the place that should be provided in which she may keep her kittens.

II. The way to treat little kittens: how to lift them; letting their eyes alone when they are very young; taking care that the kittens are not fondled too much.

TAKING CARE OF A CANARY

I. The food that should be given a canary: seeds; other foods.

II. The bird's bath: time; warmth of water.

III. The care of the cage: placing it away from drafts of air and high enough to be out of danger from cats; keeping the cage clean.

[Beginning a new paragraph]

4. The directions in Exercise 1 for taking care of a dog are written in two paragraphs. The first paragraph tells about feeding a dog. What does the second paragraph tell about?

5. How many topics are there in the outline for a talk on *Taking Care of a Cat with Kittens?* In how many paragraphs should the report be written?

6. In how many paragraphs should the report on *Taking Care of a Canary* be written?

[Written composition]

7. Choose a or b:

a. With the help of one of the outlines in Exercise 3 write a paper.

b. Write a paper telling how you have cared for some pet at home.

Be careful to begin a new paragraph with each change of topic.

[Making a report]

8. Read your report to make sure that it is correct; then, after handing your paper to your teacher, give your talk to the class.

4. Some Unexpected Letters

[Written composition]

1. Pet animals must often wish that they could speak and so express their opinions of the way in which they are neglected at times and allowed to suffer. Many of them, if they could, would write letters like this one:

The Old Barn at Dorothy's
January 15, 1927

Dear Dorothy,

   Do come home as soon as possible.   I am very unhappy.   Last night no one remembered to let me into the shed and I had to sleep under the piazza.   I nearly froze my paws.   My plate has not been washed since you went away.   Please come home.   I am sure I need you more than your cousin does.

Your loving cat,
Tabby

2. Plan a lesson period in which you all read letters that you have written for some neglected pet, such as the following:

> 1. A dog whose master forgets to feed him
> 2. A neglected rabbit or canary
> 3. Nobody's cat
> 4. A horse that is left standing in the cold without a blanket
> 5. A puppy that has been punished for getting into mischief
> 6. A cat that objects to having her kittens handled roughly

3. How will you make sure that your letter is not only interesting but also correctly written?

5. For the Story Hour.   Animal Heroes

I

1. Dogs are noted for the heroism that they have shown in rescuing children from drowning, in helping on the battle-field, and in defending their masters when they are attacked by wild animals. Wild creatures, including birds, have often proved themselves heroic in the defense of their young.

2. Tell which of these stories you have heard, and then name others like them:

Nello and Petrasche   Mother Partridge and the Fox
St. Bernard Dogs and the   Raggylug and the Black Snake
   Mountain Travelers   Gelert and the Wolf

[Learning to study]

3. The story given on page 61 tells of a brave deed done by a little gray dog:

A BRAVE DOG

Many years ago there lived a poor wood cutter named Jacques. He had built a rude cabin in the depth of the forest and there he dwelt with his wife and two small children, Jean and Marie. The children had, as their constant playmate, a good-natured little gray-coated dog.

One winter evening Jacques did not return from his work in the forest at the usual time, and the children, unknown to their mother, set out down the forest path to meet him, accompanied by the dog. Reaching home by another route a few minutes later, Jacques was alarmed at the absence of the children, and, guessing what they had done, started out to find them, carrying his axe with him. As the forest was at this season of the year infested with wolves, he was filled with fear for the safety of his children.

The wood cutter had not gone far when he heard the frightened cries of the children and the angry barking of the dog. Hurrying with all speed to the spot from which the sounds came, he found the children crouching in terror at the foot of a tree, and the dog courageously attacking a huge gray wolf, which threatened to destroy them. With a blow of his axe, Jacques killed the wolf; and, gathering little Jean and Marie in his arms, he turned homeward with gratitude in his breast. The little gray-coated dog, though severely wounded in his desperate battle with the wolf, soon recovered; and, during the rest of his life, he was regarded as a hero in the household.

4. Tell what impressed you most in the story and then be ready to give other facts.[1]

5. Try, without re-reading the story, to tell in a single sentence what each paragraph is about.

[Ending a story]

6. You have often read other stories of dogs res-

[1] See the footnote on page 47.

cuing children.   Think of a good ending for this one:

THE RESCUE

Eleanor and her dog Prince were passing a pond where some children were bathing.   One had swum some distance from the shore.   Eleanor heard a scream and saw a hand go up.   She could not swim; neither could the other children.   What was to be done?   The thought flashed across her mind that, although she could not swim, her dog could.   She picked up a stone and threw it to the spot where she had seen the hand.

II

[Planning a story hour]

7. Plan a story hour in which your class gives stories of animal heroes. Ask some of the children to look up stories like those named on page 60; ask others to tell by relay the story given of *A Brave Dog* on page 61, and others to tell original stories like the one called *The Rescue* started above, or to give a report of some book that they have read recently.

8. In making a book report, choose a story like *Black Beauty*, *A Dog of Flanders*, or *Moufflon;* or show your class *The Pet Book* by Miss Comstock. In planning your talk, use one of the suggestions given in Exercise 10, page 37.   Try in a few sentences to give an idea of the book without telling the story.

6. Review and Summary

I. Pronunciation and Meaning of Words

1. Show how to pronounce each word printed

in italics and then use it in a sentence of your own:

1. The *mischievous* puppy carried off his master's shoes.
2. The *neglected* cat slept out in the cold.
3. The shepherd dog is an *intelligent* dog.
4. A St. Bernard dog makes a *faithful* watchdog.
5. A dog is more *affectionate* than a cat.

2. Review the pronunciation of the words in Exercise 2, pages 17, 29, and in Exercise 3, page 51, by holding a contest. Divide your class into two sections and see which section can go through the words with the fewer errors. Have one word pronounced by a person on one side and the next word by some one on the other side. Keep the score on the board.

II. Abbreviations

3. In the letter on page 65, the abbreviation *W. Va.* stands for *West Virginia*. For what month does the abbreviation *Oct.* stand? What mark is placed after an abbreviation?

4. Tell for what each of these abbreviations stands and then learn the abbreviations that you do not already know:

N.	Jan.	Oct.	St.	Mr.	Hon.
S.	Feb.	Nov.	Ave.	Mrs.	Gen.
E.	Aug.	Dec.	Av.	Dr.	Col.
W.	Sept.		Rd.	Rev.	Lt.

III. The Heading of a Letter

5. Notice the following heading for a letter. Where are capitals used? How is the heading punctuated?

308 N. Poplar St., Ellensburg, Wash.
Jan. 21, 1929

6. Keep these rules in mind as you write your own address and the present date:

Use capital letters for all proper names and abbreviations for them.
Use a period after each abbreviation.
Use commas to separate the parts of an address.
Use commas to separate the parts of a date.

7. Write other headings for letters.

IV. Three Kinds of Letters

8. Read the following; then tell which letter is written to a friend, which is to an acquaintance, and which is a business letter. What differences do you find in the beginnings and endings?

Charleston, West Virginia
October 18, 1927

Dear Margaret,

At last I have the puppy for which I have been saving my money so long. You should see him; he is so fat, so affectionate, and so full of mischief. Can't you come over after school tonight?

With love,
Dorothy

Charleston, West Virginia
October 20, 1927

My dear Mrs. Brown,

I am very sorry that my puppy ran away yesterday and frightened your chickens. I will try to keep him at home after this and out of mischief.

Sincerely yours,
Dorothy Smith

Charleston, W. Va.
Oct. 25, 1927

A. G. Spalding and Brothers,
New York, N. Y.
Dear Sirs:
You will find enclosed a postal order for one dollar and twenty-five cents ($1.25) in payment for a dog collar. Please send the one numbered 14 in your catalogue. The collar should be thirteen inches in length and should be marked Laddie Smith.

Yours truly,
Dorothy Smith

9. Choose a or b:

a. Study the first letter in Exercise 8; then close your book and write it. Study the other letters one at a time and try, without looking at the book, to make perfect copies of them.

b. Write three letters of your own about a pet. Make one of them a business letter.

10. Write your letters with the directions on page 294 in mind.

V. Writing for the Class Diary

11. Be ready to talk over with your class subjects for stories and news items that might be used in writing a report for the class diary.

12. In preparing a story which you think might be used, you are to show that this half year you have learned to select a good subject, to keep to one point, and to tell enough to make the point clear. Of course you will write in separate and complete sentences and use correct English.

13. After writing your paper, what care will you take to make sure that it is correct in every way?

7. Using Words Correctly — Review for the First Half Year [1]

Test A.   Second Form.   Ten Common Errors

Copy and complete these sentences, filling the blanks with words given below Number 4:

1. The girls ——— their work neatly.
2. The boys ——— a race.
3. The ship ——— from across the ocean.
4. The sailors ——— an iceberg.

done	ran	came	seen
did	run	come	saw

Copy the answers, filling the blanks with words from below Number 8:

5. Is it your sister who has my geography?   No, it isn't ———.
6. Where did you and Mary go?   Mary and ——— went to a concert.
7. Where did you and your brother go?   ——— and ——— went on a picnic.
8. Where did you and your sister go?   ——— and ——— went to New York on a visit.

her   she   I   me   he   him

In completing the following answers, use words that make sense:

9. Why isn't Fred reading?   He ——— no book.
10. Have you his reader?   No, I ——— it.

Test B.   Second Form.   Giving Words their Right Meaning

With the help of the words given below the test, show in each case what the person should have said. Copy only what is said, not who says it.

[1] See the Teachers' Manual for an alternative test.

1. Man (speaking to carpenter): You have done the job ———.

2. Boy (asking permission of his father): ——— I go to the ball game?

3. Teacher (to pupil): ——— your book home to-night and ——— it to school in the morning.

4. Girl (teasing her mother): ——— me go to the movies, please.

5. Mother (to a little child): You must ——— down and take a nap.

6. Mary (speaking to her teacher): ——— I go home now?

good	may	take	leave	lay	will
well	can	bring	let	lie	shall

Test C. Second Form. Telling What Happened

Copy the second statement in each exercise, using a form of the word printed in italics to complete it:

1. The campers *saw* a bear. The campers had ——— a bear.

2. The boys *threw* away their knapsacks. The boys had ——— away their knapsacks.

3. The children *gave* the lost dog some food. The children had ——— the lost dog some food.

4. The caravan *went* east. The caravan had ——— east.

5. A wind storm *came* from the north. A wind storm had ——— from the north.

6. The tent pole *broke*. The tent pole was ———.

7. The boy *wrote* a report of a ball game. The boy had ——— a report.

Chapter V

FAMOUS PICTURES AND STORIES

1. Something to Do

[Planning talks]

1. With the help of the last four chapters you have been learning how to give short talks. From day to day, as you follow the suggestions in this chapter, plan to keep in practice with the earlier work. Be ready to give news items, stories of work and play, opinions of books that you have been reading, and to tell funny stories about little children.

2. To aid your class with the work in this chapter, try to find famous pictures of children and the stories that go with them. Use this list to help you:

> The Pied Piper — Kaulbach
> The Boyhood of Raleigh — Millais
> The Princes in the Tower — Millais
> James Watt — Neal
> Mozart and his Sister — Schneider
> Prince Arthur and Hubert — Yeames
> Where Did You Last See Your Father? — Yeames

[Sending an order]

3. Some of the pictures that you want you will find in your readers and histories. Others may be had for a cent or two apiece by ordering them from a picture house that supplies pictures for schools.

4. Use the business letter on page 65 to help you in planning a letter ordering pictures.

2. Secret Practice

[Conversation]

1. On page 71 there is a picture of a little boy who became a famous musician. You must wonder why he is playing in the dark and in his night clothes. This story will explain it.

> Handel was a great musician who lived a little over two hundred years ago. As a boy he showed great talent for music. When he was eight years old he could play an organ, a clavichord, or old-fashioned piano, a violin, and a horn. In spite of this talent his father, who wished him to become a lawyer, had all musical instruments taken from the house. Handel, however, managed to have a clavichord put into the garret, where it was hidden safely out of sight. At night, when the family was asleep, he stole quietly away to the garret and practiced his music. His father and mother often heard mysterious sounds at night and wondered what they were.

2. Be ready to tell one thing that you learned from the story; let your classmates tell others.[1]

3. Judging from the picture, what do you think Handel's father and mother decided to do one evening when they heard the mysterious sounds? What did they find in the attic? How did they feel when they first saw Handel playing on the hidden clavichord? What do you think they decided to do when they found how much Handel wished to become a musician?

[Choosing the right word]

4. What word in Exercise 1 describes the sound heard at night? What word shows that Handel went quietly to the garret to play?

[1] See the footnote on page 47.

5. Which of the following words describes the look on Handel's face when his father, his mother, and the rest of the family burst in upon him.

surprised frightened startled guilty ashamed alarmed

6. Suggest a word that describes the look on the mother's face.

7. What idea of the father do you get from the way he stands? Is he gentle or stern? Easy-going or strict? Full of fun or serious?

In all of your talks try to use words that tell exactly what you mean.

8. To make your class feel what a serious situation young Handel found himself in, you may use one of these suggestions and plan a talk:

a. Choose some one as a partner. One person is to tell the part of the story given in Exercise 1; the other one, with the help of the picture, is to go on with the story.

b. Pretend that you are one of the persons in the picture. Announce who you are and tell what happened.

c. Be ready to tell from your own experience how hard a person must work in order to play a piano or other instrument well.

9. Instead of using one of the plans given in Exercise 8, you may, if you prefer, look up some other story about Handel or one about another famous musician and make a report to the class.

[Written exercise]

10. Write a story, weaving into it as many as possible of the words given in the list in Exercise 5. Show the meaning of each.

After a painting by Margaret I. Dicksee

3. Listening to Voices

I

[Learning to study]

1. Joan of Arc was born over five hundred years ago, but she is so beloved by the people of France that artists still paint pictures and make statues of her. If you do not already know what she did for her country, this story will help you to find out:

JOAN OF ARC

When Joan of Arc was a young girl, there was constant warfare in France. Battles were fought, towns and cities were burned, and the people robbed. Joan, as she tended her sheep, longed to save her country from the soldiers of the enemy, who were causing so much trouble. She dreamed about saving France and prayed about it until she seemed to hear voices saying, "Put on the armor of a soldier, carry the French banner, and lead the French army to victory."

With this message in her mind Joan went to the king and said, "Gracious King, God has sent me to deliver France from her enemies. I pray you, let me lead forth the army."

The king was amazed at her request and refused to grant it, but Joan persisted. Finally, after she had visited him a second time, the king believed that she had been sent by God, so he gave her permission to do as she wished.

Dressed in white armor and mounted on a prancing black horse, Joan led the soldiers forth. Because she was both wise and brave and because the soldiers had confidence in her, she was able, after many hard battles, to win a victory which saved France from her enemies. But Joan herself was taken prisoner. She was accused of witchcraft by evil men and burned at the stake. Thus it was that, in saving her country, Joan lost her own life.

2. What impressed you most about the story
of Joan of Arc?   Be ready to tell one other interesting fact that you learned.[1]

3. The first paragraph in the story tells of the
voices heard by Joan.   Try without re-reading the
story to tell the subject of each of the other paragraphs.

4. In studying the picture, what do you notice
first of all?   What suggests that Joan is listening to
voices of angels?   What in the picture shows that
Joan is a peasant girl used to tending sheep?

[Choosing the right word]

5. Which of the following words are the best to
use in describing what Joan is doing in the picture?
Which describe the figures above her?

thinking   imagining   listening   dreaming
shining   angelic   saintly   heavenly

6. Give words that describe the character of Joan
of Arc.

[Group story]

7. As your teacher writes for you, tell her the story
suggested by the picture.   First think of a good beginning.   As you dictate the story sentence by sentence, try to choose words that exactly express your
meaning.

[Other stories]

8. When the story is finished, ask some one to
read it so that you may all enjoy it; then in your

[1] See footnote, page 47.

next lesson be ready to do one of the following things:

> a. Tell the group story, including in it any improvements that occur to you.
>
> b. Make the story in Exercise 1 clear to your class by telling it in your own words.
>
> c. Describe a scene suggested by the story.
>
> d. Find in some other book a picture or story of Joan of Arc. Use it for a talk.
>
> e. Tell the story of some other great hero or heroine.

II

[Practice in placing quotation marks]

9. Find in the first paragraph of the story on page 73, the exact words spoken to Joan of Arc. What marks set them off?

10. Be ready to write the following sentences on the blackboard and to explain the placing of the quotation marks used:

> 1. Joan of Arc said to the King, "Gracious King, God has sent me to deliver France from her enemies."
>
> 2. To her soldiers she said, "I will lead you forth, and God will help you win a victory."

11. Study the sentences in Exercise 10 and then practice writing them until you can write them correctly with your book closed.

4. For the Story Hour. Famous Pictures and their Stories

Plan a story hour in which different members of the class come prepared to report on the work suggested on page 68. Some may show pictures and describe them; others may tell the stories that go with the pictures.

5. Review, Summary, and Practice

I. Pronunciation and Meaning of Words

1. Pronounce each word in italics and then show its meaning by using it in a sentence of your own:

> *Mysterious* sounds came from the attic.
> The parents were *alarmed*.
> Joan of Arc won a *victory* for France.
> Two *innocent* princes were put to death.
> Their uncle was a *cruel* man.

2. Make sure that you can pronounce each of the following words correctly; then use them in sentences telling about your lessons:

geography	arithmetic	poem
history	reading	poetry

3. Give words that can be used in place of *is fine*.

> The picture of Joan of Arc *is fine*.

II. Review. Singular Words Showing Ownership

4. In writing a story, you often need to use words expressing ownership. Notice the words printed in italics:

> The *prince's* hand was placed on his *brother's* shoulder.

5. When words like *prince* or *brother* are used to show ownership, they are written with an apostrophe and an *s* ('s).

6. Point out the words showing ownership:

The king's crown	Handel's violin
The uncle's cruel deed	Joan of Arc's banner
The prince's fear	The commander's victory

7. Write on the board a sentence in which you use a word showing ownership.

8. As your teacher reads you the group of words in Exercise 6, write in each case the word showing ownership. Later open your book and correct your paper.

9. Write ten or more sentences containing words showing ownership.

III. Plural Words Showing Ownership

10. Tell which word in italics means one boy and which means more than one:

The *boy's* mother was ready to help.
The *boys'* mother was ready to help.

With plural words ending in *s* the apostrophe to show ownership is placed after the *s*.

11. Notice the difference in meaning of the words printed below that show ownership. Use the plural ones in sentences.

The soldier's gun	The girl's playground
The soldiers' guns	The girls' playground
The officer's quarters	The scout's knapsack
The officers' quarters	The scouts' knapsack

12. Copy the following sentences, writing after each a sentence that contains a plural word showing ownership.

Example: The boy's hat was new. The boys' hats were new.

1. The artist's picture was hung in a gallery. The ——— pictures ———.
2. The musician's violin was new.
3. The prisoner's room was small.
4. A man found the pirate's gold.
5. The sailor's chest was heavy.
6. The beggar's cap was old.
7. The soldier's uniform was ragged.

IV. Quotation Marks and the Apostrophe

13. Read the sentences in Exercise 14. Could you write them and have them correct in every way? What rules for the apostrophe should you keep in mind? Where should you use quotation marks?

14. Write these sentences with your book closed:

1. The Piper's face fell, and he cried,
   "No trifling! I can't wait, decide!"
2. The lame boy used often to say,
   "It's dull in our town since my playmates left!
   I can't forget that I'm bereft
   Of all the pleasant sights they see
   Which the Piper also promised me."

15. Write an illustration for each of these rules:

Use an apostrophe in a contraction to show that letters have been omitted.

Use an apostrophe and an *s* at the end of a singular word showing ownership.

In plural words ending in *s* place the apostrophe showing ownership after the *s*.

Use quotation marks to enclose words that are quoted as spoken.

V. Writing for the Class Diary

16. Think out carefully a news item or a story for the class diary. Tell it to the class, ask for suggestions, and then write it.

17. Before submitting your paper to your teacher, what care will you take to be certain that it is correctly written?

6. Using Words Correctly

Test D. First Form. Speaking of One or More

Copy and complete, using *is* or *are:*

1. Tom and Henry ———— members of the Boy Scouts.
2. There ———— four new members in the patrol.
3. One of them ———— twelve years old.
4. The others ———— older.

Copy and complete, using *was* or *were:*

5. Where ———— the new books put?
6. My geography and note book ———— at home.
7. On holidays there ———— no lessons for the children to learn.
8. The desk behind the others ———— mine.

Read the first question in each exercise; then copy and complete the second question:

9. *Hasn't* Alice gone?   ———— the boys gone?
10. *Aren't we* early?   ———— I ———— early?
11. *Don't* the boys study?   ———— Tom study?
12. *Was* Frank at school?   ———— you at school?

Any one whose record on the test is not perfect should use the Practice Exercises beginning on page 274.

Chapter VI

HOME OCCUPATIONS AND ENTERPRISES

1. Being Helpful at Home

[Conversation — Making plans]

Almost every boy and girl is skillful in helping with the work at home. Some are good at answering the telephone or doorbell; others can be trusted to look after younger children or to go on important errands; and still others are good at cooking, or helping in the care of the house, the walks, the garden, the lawn, a car, or the garage.

Name some of the things that you have done which you think some one else will like to try. Perhaps, if you like to cook, you can tell about making a special kind of candy; it may be that you have found a way of helping in the care of an automobile; or that you have learned of other ways of giving your father, mother, brothers, and sisters pleasant surprises.

Later, after trying out what others suggest, be ready from day to day to make a report of your experiences.

2. Using a Telephone

[Conversation]

1. The little girl shown in the picture is telephoning the doctor about her dolls, who are ill. What do you think she is saying?

2. What conversations do you carry on when you play at telephoning?

3. How do you sometimes help at home with the real telephone?

[Courtesy in telephoning]

4. Find out from this account in what ways Mary was careful when she answered the telephone.

When the telephone bell rang, Mary took the receiver from the hook, held it close to one ear, and then with her mouth near the mouthpiece, said "Hello. This is Mary Pratt."

When the person on the line asked, "Is your mother at home?" Mary answered, "Yes, I will call her."

To make it possible for her mother to talk with the person telephoning, Mary was careful to leave the receiver off the hook.

5. One way of being courteous in using the telephone is to answer it promptly. Try to think of at least three other ways.

6. Tell what you would do and say:

    a. The telephone rings.   Some one asks for your father who is at his place of business.

    b. The telephone rings.   Some one asks for some member of your family who is at home, but who cannot come to the telephone.

[Giving a talk or a dialogue]

7. With the help of one of these suggestions plan a talk or a dialogue several sentences in length:

    a. Tell a story of how you help at home with the telephone.

    b. Give directions for finding a number in a telephone directory.

    c. Give directions for being courteous in telephoning.

    d. Use a plan of your own, or one of these plans, and carry on a "telephone" conversation with some one in your room.   Use either a toy telephone or a mouthpiece and a receiver made from rolls of paper.

    Inquire about a dog that you have lost.

    Ask a friend's opinion of a book.

    Ask for directions for making candy.

    Telephone to the police about a burglar.

8. After listening to the talks, mention some of the best ideas about telephoning that you gained.

3. Answering the Doorbell

I

[Conversation — Courtesy at the door]

1. To be courteous to a visitor, a person should answer the doorbell promptly. What can he say by way of greeting? Why, in speaking to an older person, should a child, whenever he can, address a visitor by name?

2. Find four ways in which John was courteous to his mother's friend.

> When the doorbell rang, John went to the door promptly and opened it.   To Mrs. Smith, who was at the door, John said, "Good morning, Mrs. Smith," and then waited for her to speak.
> After greeting John by saying, "Good morning, John," Mrs. Smith asked, "Is your mother in?"
> John answered, "Yes, Mrs. Smith.   Will you come in and sit down?   I will call her."

3. Tell how to complete this conversation in a way that is courteous:

> Margaret (answering the doorbell): Good morning.
> Paper boy: Good morning.   I have come to collect money for the paper.
> Margaret: How much is it, please?
> Paper boy:
> Margaret:
> Paper boy:

4. What could you say to an agent from whom your mother does not care to buy?   To the postman who has a registered letter to be signed for?   To a neighbor who has come to complain of the mischief done by your dog?   To a friend who is returning a stray kitten?

[Written composition]

5. To help your class work out courteous ways of speaking, choose a or b:

> a. Copy and complete the conversation started in Exercise 3.
> b. Make up a front door conversation or a telephone conversation of your own and write it.   You may, if you

wish, pretend that a doctor, a neighbor, or a favorite aunt is either at the door or talking with you by telephone.

II

[Setting off the name of the person addressed]

6. Notice that the words in italics in the following sentences are not so necessary as others to the meaning of each sentence and for this reason they are set off by commas. These are the names of the person spoken to, or addressed.

> When are you coming to see me, *Mary?*
> *Frank*, will you stop for me on your way to school?

7. Find the name of the person spoken to or addressed:

1. John, you must take your book with you.
2. Elizabeth, when will you return home?
3. Will you wait for me, Ruth?

8. In copying this conversation from an old fairy story, where should you use commas?   Explain:

> Gretel: Look, Hansel, at the little house made of sugar and cake.
> Hansel: I will eat a piece of the roof, Gretel, and you can have some of the window.
> Witch: Nibble, nibble, little mouse.
> Who is nibbling at my house?

[Setting off *yes, no, please, thank you*]

9. Find the words set off by commas:

1. How much is it, please?
2. No, I cannot leave home.
3. Yes, I shall be glad to go.
4. My mother is better, thank you.

The word *please* in making a request and the words *yes*, *no*, *thank you*, in answering a question are set off by one or more commas.

10. Give sentences of your own showing how to use *please*, *no*, *yes*, and *thank you* in the way they are used in Exercise 9.

11. With your book closed, practice writing the sentences in Exercises 7 and 9 until you can write them correctly; then write others like them.

12. Read your conversation (see Exercise 5) to make sure that you have used commas where they are needed.

13. After your teacher has looked through the conversations written by the class, perhaps she will ask to have some of them read as dialogues with different children taking the parts.

4. Helping with the Cleaning

I

[Conversation]

1. Most boys and girls like to see a house clean and in order, and most of them find ways of helping to keep it so. Name one thing that you sometimes do, and other tasks for which you are regularly responsible.

2. Tell which of these questions you can answer:

What is done in cleaning a kitchen floor?   In cleaning a rug?   In dusting a room?   In washing windows?   In polishing silver?   In scouring a knife?   In cleaning doorsteps?   In putting a basement or cellar in order? In using an electric washer?   In ironing handkerchiefs? In giving a dog a bath?

3. Your class will be interested in trying out some of the things mentioned in Exercise 2 that you have done.   First decide what you would like to tell.

[Using a plan in giving a talk]

4. In telling how to clean a kitchen floor, you might tell (1) what to use; (2) what to do first; and (3) what to do after that.   Why should the directions be given in the right order?

5. What plan could you follow in giving directions for polishing silver?   In telling how to clean a bicycle?

6. Think out a plan for the talk you would like to give.

7. Have the different members of the class tell their plans, and let the class decide which talks they would like to hear first.

8. After listening to the talks, tell which speakers gave you ideas that you are going to try at home.

II

[Setting off words in a list]

9. First name the words that form the lists in each sentence; then tell what mark separates the words:

At the grocery John bought soap, blueing, and starch.
At the bakery he got bread, cookies, a pie, and a cake.

10. Remember to use commas to separate the words in a sentence that form a list.

11. Tell where commas belong:

Helen Elizabeth and Mary were ready to help their mother.   They got out a broom dustpan and dust cloth. Soon they were busy sweeping dusting and setting things in order.

Fred found Frank Tom and Harry in the garage. They were hunting for screws bolts a hammer and a screw-driver.

Ruth ironed the sheets pillowcases and towels. Mother ironed the tablecloths the shirt waists and the dresses.

Helen Elizabeth and Tom helped get dinner.

Notice that in giving a list only one *and* is used.   It is the custom to say *Helen, Elizabeth, and Tom*.   It is not the custom to say *Helen, and Elizabeth, and Tom*.

12. Use each of the following groups of words in a sentence:

1. coffee oatmeal eggs toast
2. sprinkled rolled put into a basket
3. rinsed wrung hung out
4. plates knives forks tumblers
5. scrubbing-brush hot water soap
6. saw hammer nails
7. hoe rake spade
8. sugar butter eggs flour

[Written exercise]

13. Copy the sentences in Exercise 11, putting in commas where they are needed; and then write sentences containing the lists given in Exercise 12.

5. A Boy's Birthday Supper

[Giving details for clearness]

1. Name some of the kinds of food that boys like to eat at a birthday supper.

2. Give, if you can, the missing words:

(1) Before baking ———, mother rolls the dough out flat and thin and cuts it into circles. She places the circles of dough in tins and puts them into the oven. Some times she sprinkles a little sugar over them or places a raisin on each.

(2) For ———, mother makes a sweet custard and mixes it with cream. This mixture she puts into a can which she sets in a wooden pail. She packs ice around the can and some salt, and then turns a handle which is fastened to a dasher. The dasher stirs the custard and cream.

(3) In making ———, Mary mixes chocolate, sugar, and a little milk, and puts the mixture into a skillet to boil. When the ——— is done, she puts in butter and flavoring.

[Written composition]

3. Write a riddle like one of those in Exercise 2.

[Practice in writing words in a list]

4. Tell where commas belong:

In making cake mother used sugar butter milk eggs flour and baking powder.

For peanut candy Helen used sugar water and shelled peanuts.

For his birthday supper Fred had ice cream cake and candy.

5. Read your riddle to see that it is correctly written; then exchange it for one composed by a classmate.

6. If you can guess the riddle that you receive by exchange, and if you think it is a good one, you are to read it to the class.

6. Safety-First at Home

[Conversation]

1. Many accidents in homes come from carelessness with matches and from scalding water. Babies, of course, are fascinated by matches and by bright handles of dishes that are left within their reach.

2. Accidents from burns may often be prevented by care on the part of older boys and girls. Be ready to give your ideas of how this can be shown, and then to answer the following questions:

Where should matches be kept?

Why are safety matches better than other kinds in homes where there are little children?

How can a fire be put out when no water is at hand?

When a child's clothes catch fire, how can you smother the flames with a blanket?

How does rolling over and over help a child to put out the flames?

How can a fire alarm be given?

In what way can you prevent accidents caused by little children who reach for bright handles and spill boiling water or hot fat on themselves?

[Written composition — Gaining attention]

3. Tell how accidents from open wells, broken walks, and from rusty nails may be prevented.

4. Write a paper to read to your class in which you express your ideas of how you can help in making your own home a safe place. First try to think of an opening sentence that will make your class wish to listen to what you have to read. Think of other sentences like these:

> Of course no one wishes to have accidents at home.
> Boys and girls as well as older people can help in the prevention of accidents at home.
> In the matter of accidents an ounce of prevention is worth a pound of cure.

7. For a Quiet Hour

I

[Learning to study]

1. Long ago there lived a poet who had a tender heart and a vivid imagination. He wrote many beautiful poems like the following:

> The sun descending in the west,
>   The evening star does shine;
> The birds are silent in their nest,
>   And I must seek for mine.
>   The moon, like a flower
>   In heaven's high bower,
>   With silent delight
>   Sits and smiles on the night.

> Farewell, green fields and happy groves,
>   Where flocks have ta'en delight;
> Where lambs have nibbled, silent move
>   The feet of angels bright;

Unseen, they pour blessing
And joy without ceasing,
On each bud and blossom,
And each sleeping bosom.

They look in every thoughtless nest,
  Where birds are covered warm,
They visit caves of every beast,
  To keep them all from harm:
    If they see any weeping
    That should have been sleeping,
  They pour sleep in their head,
  And sit down by their bed.
                              WILLIAM BLAKE

2. Be ready to tell what you think the title of the poem above is, and to give reasons for your choice.

3. Each stanza in the poem contains a clear picture. What kind of night is described in the first stanza? What is pictured in the second stanza as moving silently through the fields and groves? What in the third stanza gives a feeling of loving care?

4. Select a favorite stanza, describe the scene pictured, and then read the stanza to the class.

II

[Planning a program]

5. The boys and girls in your class will enjoy giving a program of poems and quotations. How will you help with the work? If you decide to give a quotation, you may select one from the following list and memorize it. If you decide to recite a poem, you are to find one that you like and which you think others will enjoy. Make sure that you can read the poem

well; memorize it; and then, before giving it at
school, rehearse it to some one.

TRUE GREATNESS

Who says, " I will " to what is right,
 " I won't " to what is wrong,
Although a tender little child,
 Is truly great and strong.

LOVING HEARTS

He prayeth best who loveth best
 All things both great and small;
For the dear God who loveth us,
 He made and loveth all.

BE GOOD SWEET MAID

Be good, sweet maid, and let who will be clever;
 Do noble things, not dream them, all day long:
And so make Life, Death, and that vast Forever,
 One grand, sweet song.

THE HOUSE OF NEVER

They who travel with By-and-by
Soon come to the house of Never.

THE REMEDY

For every evil under the sun,
There is a remedy, or there is none.
If there be one, try to find it;
If there is none, never mind it.

A HAPPY HEART

Who will remember that skies are gray
If he carries a happy heart all day?

A MERRY HEART

Jog on, jog on, the footpath way,
　　And merrily jump the stile-a;
A merry heart goes all the day,
　　Your sad one tires in a mile-a.

8. Review and Summary

I. Pronunciation and Meaning of Words

1. Show that you have learned how to use each word printed in italics, first by pronouncing it correctly, and then by giving a sentence of your own containing it:

　　1. The boys were *courteous* to their guests.
　　2. Mother *greeted* her friend at the door.
　　3. Mary was careful to hang the telephone *receiver* on its hook.
　　4. An *accident* is often caused by a child's playing with matches.
　　5. The vacuum cleaner is run by *electricity*.

2. The following words are often mispronounced. Show how each should be said and then guard your speech against the incorrect pronunciation.

cruel	was	ask	due
jewel	wash	part	duty
towel	want	last	knew
civil	what	dance	Tuesday

3. Give at least two other words that may be used in place of *asked*.

　　The man *asked*, "Where is there a garage?"

II. The Uses of the Comma

4. Could you write a letter like the following one and have it correct in every way?

Prosser, Montana

March 8, 1928

Dear Tom,

    Last evening Father gave me a great surprise. When I reached home from school, Mother said, "Billy, go out to the garage, please.   Your father wishes to see you."   Out I went and there I found a new bicycle.   I was so pleased that I tried to dance, whistle, and shout all at once.   Can't you come over and see it?

Your old friend,

Billy

5. The comma after *school* in the second line is used to show a slight change of thought.   Give the reasons for the other commas.

6. Close your book and make a copy of the letter in Exercise 3.   Be careful to observe these rules:

Use a comma:

    To separate the parts of an address.

    To separate the parts of a date.

    To set off words like *Dear Tom* at the beginning of a letter and *Your old friend* at the end of a letter.

    To separate words in a list.

    To set off the name of a person spoken to or addressed.

    To set off independent words like *yes, no, please, thank you*.

    To set off the exact words used by a speaker.

7. Choose a, b, or c:

    a. Write a letter to your teacher telling of new ways of helping at home that you have tried lately.

    b. Pretend that a cousin who is underweight and not very strong has written asking you what he can do to grow strong and well.   Write him a letter.

    c. Write a letter to a boy (or girl) who would like to know a good way of earning money with which to buy a fountain pen or some other article which he would like to own.

III. Writing for the Class Diary

8. With the stories in mind that you have given in the last few weeks, decide what you would like to submit in writing for the class diary. Be ready also to dictate a group story to your teacher as she writes on the board for you, and later to choose members of the class to copy it.

9. Before submitting your story, read it through, first to make sure that you have written it in separate sentences, and next for spelling, the use of capitals, and marks of punctuation.

9. Using Words Correctly

Test E.   First Form.   Words Often Confused

Copy and complete these exercises, using in each sentence a word that sounds either exactly like the one in italics or somewhat like it:

1. The boys found that in *their* boat ——— were no oars.
2. In *our* flag there ——— thirteen stripes.
3. The box was ——— small *to* hold ——— pounds of candy.
4. We found that *two* of the chains were ——— old ——— be used.
5. We *knew* that we needed ——— books.

Any one making an error in the test should use the Practice Exercises beginning on page 277.

Chapter VII — CURIOUS HOMES

1. Something to Do

[Making plans]

1. We are all of us interested in befriending birds and other wild creatures. In winter we put out suet and crumbs to prevent the birds from starving. In the early spring we build bird houses for them and later do what we can to keep cats and other enemies away from the young birds. At all times we try to learn all that we can about the habits of wild creatures and the kinds of homes they build; and, as we observe the birds and other little friends, we are careful never to disturb their young.

2. To help your class with the study of curious homes, try to do at least one of the following things:

1. Take a "census" of the homes of the birds, squirrels, chipmunks, and other wild creatures living near you.
2. Bring to class a picture of a bird common in your locality. Bring also a picture of its nest and eggs.
3. Bring to class a deserted bird's nest, an empty hornet's nest, or some other curious home.
4. Be ready to make a report of any work that you have done for birds or other wild creatures in your neighborhood.
5. Look up a story about a bird or an insect to tell during the Story Hour.
6. Bring to class books telling about birds, insects, and other living things.

3. Long ago, when our country was a wilderness and travel was dangerous, John Audubon traveled

on foot and by horseback over the country studying the birds and their habits. In honor of his courage and the work that he did, a society for the protection of birds calls itself the Audubon Society.

4. If you would like to know what the society is doing, you may use the following letter to help you in writing for a circular of information:

The Forestville School
Chicago, Illinois
April 30, 1927

The Audubon Society
    66 Newbury Street
        Boston, Massachusetts
Dear Sirs:
        Our class is studying birds. We should like to know something about the Junior Audubon Society. Will you please send us a circular of information?

Yours truly,
The Fifth Grade

5. Your class may wish to join the Audubon Society or to form a nature club of your own. Perhaps, too, you would like to keep the stories that you tell in your next lessons, and to bind them in a little book.

2. Building a Nest

[Conversation]

1. Early in the spring, after mating, birds begin to build their nests. The outside of the nest is often made of sticks or grass. The inside is lined to make it soft and comfortable. Be ready to tell in what places you have seen nests and what birds you have seen building them.

2. The birds pictured on this page are robins. Tell why the nest was placed in the crotch between the branches of a tree.

3. The outside of a robin's nest is made of twigs. How are these sticks held together?   With what is the nest usually lined?

4. With the help of this paragraph find how the red-headed woodpecker builds its nest.

WORKING BY TURNS

The red-headed woodpecker selects, by preference, a partly decayed tree in which to excavate a hole for its nest because it is easier to dig in old dead wood and the sawdust and chips make a softer lining than green wood. The male and female take turns in this hollowing-out process.   The one that is off duty is allowed "twenty minutes for refreshments," consisting of grubs, beetles, fruit, and nuts.   At a loving call from its mate in the hollow tree, it returns promptly to perform its share of the work when the carefully observed "time" is up. The heap of sawdust at the bottom of the hollow will eventually cradle from four to six glossy white eggs.

Adapted from *Bird Neighbors*, by Neltje Blanchan, by permission of the publishers, Doubleday, Page & Co.

5. Tell one thing that you found in reading Exercise 4.[1]

[Accuracy in observation]

6. John Audubon and all other great nature lovers have been careful observers. Try to give the facts called for here and thus show that, in observing the birds in your neighborhood, you too have kept your eyes open.

 1. The favorite place for a sparrow's nest
 2. Where woodpeckers build their nests
 3. The color of a robin's egg
 4. To what common bird the large, rickety nest belongs that is built high up in a tree in the woods or in a pasture
 5. What bird builds its nest in a deserted chimney
 6. Where kingfishers build their nests
 7. The usual color of a bird that builds its nest on the ground

[Using a plan in giving a talk]

7. If you were to tell the story in Exercise 4, you might tell first about the place the woodpeckers choose for a home, how the birds work by turns, and then what will be cradled in the nest. What plan might you keep in mind in telling about a robin's nest? In showing how an oriole's nest differs from a robin's nest?

8. In preparing a talk, choose b, c, or d, if it is possible, and have a nest or picture to show; otherwise, choose a.

 a. Be ready to make the story in Exercise 4 clear by telling it in your own words.

[1] See the footnote on page 47.

b. Use one of the plans worked out in Exercise 7 and think what to say.

c. Use a plan of your own and think out a talk.

d. Make up a story about a bird with which you are familiar.   Use facts that will show the habits of the bird.

9. Ask the members of the class to give the subjects of their talks and then choose the speakers you would like to hear first.

[Accuracy in retelling a story]

10. Re-read the story in Exercise 4; then, after closing your book, write the story in your own words. Try to include all the important facts and to write the story without an error.

3. A Snug Cradle

[Conversation]

1. Guess this riddle if you can:

I creep upon the ground, and the children say,
"You ugly old thing!" and push me away.

I lie in my bed and the children say,
"The fellow is dead; we'll throw him away."

At last I awake, and the children try
To make me stay, as I rise and fly.

2. Every one admires a butterfly with its delicate wings so gayly colored, but not every one admires the caterpillar that spins the cocoon from which the butterfly comes.   Be ready to tell in a clear sentence something that you have noticed about each.

3. Here are words that might be used in describing

Adult
Caterpillar

Papilio asterias

Chrysalis

a butterfly's wings.   Try to think of at least three others.

delicate	veined	prettily marked
gauzy	dusty	gayly colored
dainty	powdered	beautifully decorated

4. What words can be used in describing a co-coon?

[Giving details for clearness]

5. With the help of one of these suggestions give a talk:

a. Tell the story of how a caterpillar changed into a butterfly.

b. Explain the riddle in Exercise 1; then give it from memory.

c. Tell what you have observed about caterpillars and butterflies; the kinds that you have seen; when and where you have seen them; and what they were doing.

d. Show the class a butterfly, a moth, or a cocoon, and describe it.

e. Give a report on the silkworm.

Plan your talk carefully. Show that you have been a good observer and can express your ideas in thoughtful sentences, and also that you can choose words that exactly fit your meaning.

6. After you have heard the talks by others, you are to help the class in deciding which ones should be written for the class book on *Curious Homes*.

[Review. Punctuation]

7. Explain the use of quotation marks in the riddle in Exercise 1; then with your book closed write as much of the riddle as you can remember.

4. A Spider's Web

[Conversation]

1. The wheel-shaped spider's web pictured here has thirty-two spokes, and at its widest part it has over twenty-five cross lines. Where do spiders usually build such webs? Why do they spin the

threads so close together? Of what use are the spokes when the spider is at the center of the web?

2. The spider has no real home, but it is usually found near its web. Give a reason for its keeping near its web; then tell how you can prove that it does do so.

3. Be ready to tell in a single sentence some interesting fact that you have observed about spiders and their webs.

4. Which of these words describe a spider building its web? Which describe it catching flies?

persistent	cunning	wise
quick	watchful	wary
lively	industrious	noiseless

[Planning a talk]

5. If you were to tell of an experience that you have had watching a spider spinning its web, what would you plan to tell about first? Next? After that? Give your plan in a sentence or two.

6. What could be said in a talk if this sentence was used as an introduction:

The spider makes a good trap with which to catch flies.

[Oral and written composition]

7. Give a talk, using one of these suggestions:

a. Use the beginning printed in Exercise 6 and the plan that you worked out.

b. Use the plan worked out in Exercise 5 and tell about an experience that you have had watching a spider.

c. Make up a story showing the habits of a spider.

d. Describe a tarantula that sometimes comes in a

bunch of bananas.   To get information, ask questions and use books.

8. What care will you take in composing your talk?   In writing it later for the class book?

[Dividing words]

9. On page 291 are rules that you have been using in dividing words at the end of a line.   Copy the words in Exercise 4.   Use hyphens to show where each may be divided.

5. For the Story Hour.   Nature Stories and Books

I

[Learning to study]

1. The magpie is a noisy, chattering bird that somewhat resembles a jay in its disposition.   Its character is shown in the following story:

WHY THE MAGPIE'S NEST IS BADLY MADE

Once on a time, when the world was very young, the magpie was the only bird that did not know how to build a nest.   She told her trouble to the other birds and they all met to teach her.

"Place that stick there," said the blackbird.   He flew over and did it himself.

"Oh," said the magpie, "I knew that before."

"Place this stick here," said the thrush, placing it for her.

"Oh," said the magpie, "I knew that before."

The wren and the robin, the goldfinch and the chaffinch, the lark and the swallow, and many other birds went on showing her how to build the nest.   As each bit was added, the magpie said, "Oh, I knew that before."

At last when the nest was only half finished, the birds lost patience with the conceited empty-head.

"Well, Mistress Mag," cried they, flying away, "since you know all about it, you may finish the nest yourself."

That is the reason the magpie's nest is so badly made.

2. Judging from the story, what do you think was the reason why the magpie's nest is badly made?

3. With the help of the class try to recall all that happened in the story.   Each is to tell one thing[1] until all the facts have been given.

[Retelling a story]

4. Re-read the story; then tell it in a lively, enter-taining way.   Get it so well in mind that you can give it without hesitation and without using un-necessary *so*'s, *and*'s, and *why*'s.

II

[Planning a program]

5. With the help of the class plan a program of nature stories.   Ask for volunteers.   Some mem-bers of the class may read stories from the class book on *Curious Homes* or make a report on observations they have made, others may tell stories like those in the following list, and still others may make book reports.

Nature Stories

Robert Bruce and the Spider's Web
How the Mole Became Blind
King Solomon and the Bees

[1] See the footnote on page 47.

The Ant and Achilles
Mother Partridge and her Chicks
How the Chipmunk Got its Stripes

6. If you decide to make a book report, try to find a nature book, such as *The First Book of Birds* by Olive Thorne Miller, *Bird Neighbors* by Neltje Blanchan, or the *Burgess Animal Book for Children;* or select an interesting book of poems, such as the *Posy Ring, Three Years with the Poets*, or *Tree-Top and Meadow*.

6. Review and Summary

I. Pronunciation and Meaning of Words

1. Be ready first to pronounce each word printed in italics and then to show its meaning by using it in a sentence of your own:

1. Birds use their bills and claws in *weaving* sticks into their nests.
2. The humming-bird's eggs are well *protected*.
3. Caterpillars and moths build *cocoons*.
4. The butterfly spreads its *delicate* wings.
5. Spiders *anchor* their webs.

2. Review the pronunciation of words in Exercise 2, pages 76 and 93, and make a report on your success in correcting wrong pronunciation in your own speech.

3. Make sure that you can pronounce each of the following words correctly:

nature	once	standing	below
picture	scared	going	believe

II. Writing a Conversation

4. Think of a reason for the quotation marks in these sentences; also for each comma.

"Place that stick there," said the blackbird.
"Oh!" said the magpie, "I knew that before."
"Well, Mistress Mag, you may finish the nest yourself," cried the other birds.

5. As you copy the sentences in Exercise 4, keep these rules in mind:

Enclose in quotation marks all words that are quoted as spoken.

Use one or more commas to set off from the rest of the sentence all words that are quoted.

Begin a new paragraph with each change of speaker.

6. Copy and punctuate the following story:

THE TURTLE THAT COULDN'T STOP TALKING

Two geese once invited a turtle to fly with them to their home in the South
How can I asked the turtle I have no wings
That is easily managed answered the geese if you can keep your mouth closed
The next day the geese brought a stick which they held by the ends   Take the middle of the stick in your mouth and remember not to say a word they said to the turtle
The geese then sprang into the air with the turtle between them but as they flew overhead some children saw them, and cried out Oh see the turtle in the air   Look at the geese carrying a turtle by a stick   Did you ever see anything more ridiculous in your life
The turtle looked down and began to say Well if my friends carry me, what business is that of yours when he let go and fell to the earth

Adapted from *Jataka Tales*, retold by Ellen C. Babbitt, by permission of the publishers, The Century Co.

III. Writing for the Class Diary

7. In your class diary you will surely wish to have an account of the study you have been making of curious homes. Be ready to give other news items and also to tell stories that you would like to have included. By this time you should be able to write interesting reports as well as to compose excellent group stories.

8. What care can you take to make sure that your reports are written correctly?

7. Using Words Correctly

Test F. First Form. Telling What Happened

Copy the second statement in each exercise, using a form of the word printed in italics to complete it:

1. The church bell has *rung*. The church bell ———.
2. The sun had *begun* to set. The sun ——— to set.
3. The birds had *sung* their evening songs. The birds ——— their evening songs.
4. The leaves had *lain* on the ground all winter. The leaves ——— on the ground all winter.
5. The traveler had *sat* beneath the tree. The traveler ——— beneath the tree.
6. The man *drank* from the stream. The man had ——— from the stream.
7. He *ate* berries. He had ——— berries.
8. The artist *drew* a picture of the sunset. The artist had ——— a picture of the sunset.

For Practice Exercises see pages 270–274.

Chapter VIII

THE STORY OF THE AMERICAN FLAG

1. The American Flag

[Conversation]

Out on the breeze, o'er land and seas,
A beautiful banner is streaming.
Shining its stars, splendid its bars,
Under the sunshine 'tis gleaming.
Over the brave long may it wave,
Peace to the world ever bringing;
While to the stars, linked with the bars,
Hearts will forever be singing.

LYDIA COONLEY WARD

1. The American flag stands for what all Americans wish, — freedom and justice. Wherever it flies, on land or sea, it brings a message of peace and good will.

2. Tell how you know that the flag described in the stanza above is that of our own country. What wish is made? Why is it that the flag causes hearts forever to be singing?

3. Soldiers are always very careful of their treatment of the flag.   To them it stands for the country for which they are ready to fight and die.   They never dishonor it by letting it touch the ground, nor by passing it without a salute.   At sunrise when they raise the flag, they fire a cannon.   At sunset they lower it with a salute of guns.

4. In order to follow directions for displaying a flag, you need to know that the part made up of red and white stripes is called the *field*.   The stripes tell the number of colonies out of which the United States was formed.   How many stripes are there? What is the color of the larger number?

5. The stars tell how many states now form the union.   How are the stars arranged?   How many are there?

6. With which of these rules are you familiar? Be ready to give in your own words at least one of them.

The flag should be raised at sunrise and lowered at sunset.   It may be raised at other times, but should never be left out at night, except when it is under the fire of an enemy.

On Memorial Day the flag should be displayed at half-staff from sunrise until noon, and at the peak from noon until sunset.

When the flag is raised to half-staff, or half-mast, it should always be run to the peak and then lowered a distance equal to the breadth of the flag.   In retiring it, it should first be run back to the peak and then retired. It should never be allowed to touch the ground.

When the *Star-Spangled Banner* is played or sung, a person should stand and remain standing, until it is finished.

When the flag is passing on parade, or in review, if a person is walking, he should halt; if sitting, he should rise, stand at attention, and if he is a man or a boy, he should take off his hat.

[Planning an entertainment]

7. June 14, 1777, was the birthday of our flag. Before this day other flags were used. Of these flags you will learn in the next two lessons. If you wish to use the stories in an entertainment, the program on page 122 will help you in deciding what to do. For flags you can draw pictures on the blackboard or on large sheets of drawing paper. The pictures in the dictionary will show you what colors to use.

2. The First Flags Used in America

I. The Flag Carried by the Mayflower

The Cross of St. George (England)

The Cross of St. Andrew (Scotland)

The British Union (used by the Mayflower)

The British Union with a crimson field (used after 1707 in English colonies)

[Conversation]

1. We have not always had the Stars and Stripes for a flag. In the early days several colonies in America used the flag called the British Union. It was this flag that the Mayflower is supposed to have

carried and the one that was used in Jamestown for over one hundred and sixty years.

2. The British Union stood for the union of England and Scotland. What two crosses were shown in the flag?

3. At first the British Union was made with a blue background and without a crimson field. What change took place in the flag in 1707?

4. In describing the British Union, what can you say of the position of the two crosses? Of the colors in the flag?

II. Pine Tree and Rattlesnake Flags

CULPEPPER MINUTE MEN   MASSACHUSETTS NAVY .   WASHINGTON'S CRUISERS

5. Just before the Revolution, when the colonists were trying to win their freedom, many different flags were used in the North, in the South, and at sea. Tell what is pictured on those shown on this page.

6. What mottoes appear on the pine-tree flags? For what did the colonies wish? What, then, was meant by *An appeal to heaven*?

7. Tell what mottoes were printed on the rattlesnake flag. What was the meaning of *Don't tread on me*?

[Making a talk clear]

8. To make clear the story of the early flags used in America, plan a talk. Choose a, b, or c:

a. Tell the story of the British Union.

b. Give a talk describing the Pine Tree and Rattlesnake flags. Use a beginning of your own or this one:
The flags carried by the colonists before the Revolutionary War showed that they wished their freedom.

c. Find in your history or elsewhere a picture of the flag brought to America by Columbus. Describe it to your class.

9. As you listen to the talks, decide which can be used in a flag day program. Tell how the talks can be improved, and then ask to have them written.

3. Stars and Stripes

1. Since the early days in the Revolutionary War, many changes have been made in the flag. Judging from the pictures, what changes should you say have taken place in the part containing the stars? Which flag has fifteen stripes?

2. The story of the flags is given here. Try in reading each selection once to get the main facts:

THE GRAND UNION

The first flag to stand for the united colonies was the Grand Union. This flag was raised by Captain Paul Jones in December, 1775, when flags were first displayed in the new navy. It was also used a month later by George Washington when in January, 1776, he took command of the new army.

THE FIRST STARS AND STRIPES

June 14, 1777, was the birthday of the Stars and Stripes. On that day Congress voted "That the flag of the thirteen United States be thirteen stripes, alternating red and white; that the union be thirteen stars, white in a blue field, representing a new constellation."

THE STAR–SPANGLED BANNER

Before the War of 1812 two new states came into the union. For this reason two more stars and two more stripes were added to the flag, making it a flag of fifteen stars and fifteen stripes. During the war, Francis Scott Key saw this flag floating above a fort at early dawn amidst the smoke and fire of a bombardment. It was then that he wrote *The Star-Spangled Banner*, beginning with these lines:

"Oh say, can you see by the dawn's early light
What so proudly we hailed at the twilight's last
gleaming?
Whose broad stripes and bright stars, thro' the perilous fight,
O'er the ramparts we watched were so gallantly
streaming";

OLD GLORY

In 1818 Congress voted that a return should be made to the thirteen stripes and that a star should be added for each new state. This flag, which started with thirteen stars and now has forty-eight, is often called the Stars and Stripes or Old Glory.

3. Be ready to tell in turn with your classmates some one thing that you learned about each flag.

4. Test your class on Exercise 2 by asking questions like the following: When did the flag have thirteen stars? What day is called the birthday of the Stars and Stripes? What kind of flag was used in 1812?

5. Appoint committees to draw large pictures of the flags on the board or on large sheets of paper, two or three members of the class working together on each.

6. If you were to show the pictures to another class, what would you point out in that of the Grand Union? In that of the first Stars and Stripes? In that of the Star-Spangled Banner? In that of Old Glory?

[Making a talk clear]

7. In preparing a talk on the Stars and Stripes, choose one of the flags, describe it, and then in your own words tell its story. Try to make what you say so clear that a visiting class will remember it.

8. Later you are to write your talk so that if it is wanted on the program (see page 122), it will be ready for use.

4. The American Flag in France

[Conversation]

1. During the World War, when the American troops first arrived in France, they were surprised to see a number of French children kneel in the street as the American flag was carried by. Why do you think the little French children knelt at the sight of the flag?

2. This poem tells the story of what happened:

IN THE MIDST OF THEM[1]

(Why so patient, standing there,
Edouard and small Pierre.[2]
Georges, Yvette, and Marie-Claire?[2])

"When the troops come marching by,"
        (Quoth the small Pierre,)
"Mother, wilt thou lift me high,
That we see them, thou and I?"

"Mother, are they fair to see?"
        (A busy tongue — Pierre —)
"Have they little boys like me,
Left at home across the sea?"
        (Alas! alas! Pierre.)

"Mother, we have **waited** long";
        (Long, indeed, Pierre!)
"The sun has grown so hot and strong —
Surely none has done them wrong?"
        (God forbid, Pierre.)

"Mother, who did send them here?"
        (The gift of God, Pierre.)

---

[1] Copyright, 1918, by Charles Scribner's Sons.
[2] These names are pronounced: — Ad-war, Pee-air, Zhorzh, E-vet', Ma-rie-Claire'.

"But then there is no need of fear,
And on thy cheek I see a tear —"
  (*The tears of hope, Pierre.*)

Down the boulevard a cry —
A bugle note is flung on high —
The Stars and Stripes are passing by;

"The gift of God," quoth small Pierre;
His hat on breast, his curls all bare,
He knelt upon the pavement there.

(*Five small children kneeling there,
Georges, Yvette, and Marie-Claire,
Edouard and small Pierre.*)

Fairest flag of Liberty —
Carrying hope across the sea —
A little child has hallowed thee,
  And made of thee a prayer!

Margaret Bell Merrill

3. You have sometimes waited a long time for a procession to appear, so that you can understand how little Pierre felt. What were some of the questions that he asked?

4. Little Pierre is thinking of the procession. How can you tell that his mother is thinking of the long sad days of the war? What shows that she hopes that the coming of the Americans will bring victory to the French side?

5. What scene do you picture with the arrival of the troops?

[Written composition — An introduction to a poem]

6. Tell what you think could be said to help an audience understand the poem; then use one of the

following suggestions and write a paper that could be used as an introduction.

> a. Make the thought of the poem clear by writing the story in your own words.
>
> b. Describe the scene that you see in your mind when you think of the soldiers making their appearance, the eager crowd, and little Pierre and the other children kneeling.
>
> c. Tell how the poem came to be written and what it shows. (Do not tell the story.)

7. After you have heard a number of the papers, choose the one that you think would help other children most to understand the poem. Use this paper as part of your program.

5. Showing Respect for the Flag

I

[Conversation]

1. A person who has imagination sees much more than a piece of cloth when he sees the flag. He may think of the American soldiers fighting in France or he may look back to the days of the Revolution and see soldiers in ragged uniform fighting under Washington or suffering from cold and hunger. What other scenes may he picture of men serving the flag?

2. In showing respect for the flag, we are honoring the soldiers who fought for the country. Whom else are we honoring?

3. If you have ever watched a procession of soldiers and thought of all that the flag means, you can understand the thrilling scene described in this poem.

THE FLAG GOES BY

Hats off!

Along the street there comes
A blare of bugles, a ruffle of drums,
A flash of color beneath the sky;
        Hats off!
The flag is passing by!

Blue and crimson and white it shines,
Over the steel-tipped, ordered lines.
        Hats off!
The colors before us fly;
But more than the flag is passing by.

Sea-fights and land-fights, grim and great,
Fought to make and to save the State:
Weary marches and sinking ships;
Cheers of victory on dying lips;

Days of plenty and years of peace;
March of a strong land's swift increase;
Equal justice, right and law,
Stately honor and reverend awe;

Sign of a nation, great and strong
To ward her people from foreign wrong:

Pride and glory and honor, — all
Live in the colors to stand or fall.

Hats off!

Along the street there comes
A blare of bugles, a ruffle of drums;
And loyal hearts are beating high:
Hats off!
The flag is passing by!

HENRY HOLCOMB BENNETT

4. Tell what in the poem impresses you the most.

5. How do you know that a company of soldiers is passing? What do you think is the finest sight in the procession?

6. What words referring to the flag in the first and second stanzas help you to picture it?

7. What in the second stanza shows that the soldiers were carrying bayonets, or guns tipped with swords of steel, and that the men were marching in even rows?

8. What scenes are named in the third stanza to show that the flag has been carried through wars and bravely defended by soldiers?

9. How do the scenes suggested in the fourth stanza differ from those named in the third?

10. What is the flag called in the fifth stanza?

11. How does the last stanza differ from the first?

12. Re-read the poem; then, in order to make it clear to your class use one of these suggestions:

a. Tell the story of the poem in such a way that your listeners will realize that soldiers are passing with the sound of trumpet and drum and the waving of flags.

b. Give a talk naming different places where the flag is carried in time of war. Tell why, because of this, we should honor the flag.

c. Describe three scenes that a person of imagination may see when he looks at the flag.

6. Quotations. Our Flag

[Memorizing]

If you would like to have quotations given at your entertainment, you are to memorize the stanza on page 109 or one of these selections:

"When you see the flag waving in the air, it says to you: 'This is a free land.' The colors have their message too. The red says, 'Be brave'; the white says, 'Be pure'; the blue says, 'Be true.'"

"We scorn when we see the flag to be idle or mean, or false and dishonest."

"There are many flags in many lands,
    There are flags of every hue,
  But there's no flag, however grand,
    Like our own 'Red, White, and Blue.'"

"Our flag, beautiful in peace, glorious in war."

"Red, White, and Blue, wave on!
  Never may sire or son
    Thy glory mar.
  Saved to liberty,
  Honored on land and sea,
  Unsoiled forever be,
    Each stripe and star."

"The flag floats east,
The flag floats west
The skies unveil their glory,
The stripes reflect the beautiful light,
While star tells to star its story."

7. A Program for Flag Day

1. With the help of the following program complete your own and make arrangements for carrying it out:

A PROGRAM

1. Entrance of flag bearer.   The audience rises and stands at attention.   Pledging allegiance.
2. Singing — The Star Spangled Banner
3. Stories of the flag told by boys and girls as pictures are shown.
   1. The Flag Carried by the Mayflower
   2. The Pine Tree and Rattlesnake Flags
   3. The Grand Union, The First Stars and Stripes, The Star-Spangled Banner of 1812, Old Glory.
4. Our Flag and What it Means
5. The American Flag in France
6. The Treatment of the Flag
7. Poems and Quotations.   Our Flag
8. Singing America

2. In pledging allegiance[1] to the flag, you may use the following words:

I pledge allegiance to the Flag of the United States and to the Republic for which it stands, one nation, indivisible, with Liberty and Justice for all.

The pledge means that you promise to be a good citizen and to protect the rights of others.

[1] In pledging allegiance, pupils should stand at attention.

8. Review and Summary

I. Pronunciation and Meaning of Words

1. Pronounce each word printed in italics and then use it in a sentence of your own:

    1. The British Union was used by the American *colonies*.
    2. A good citizen is careful not to *dishonor* the flag.
    3. The men *saluted* the flag.
    4. The soldiers pledged *allegiance* to the country.

2. To make sure that you can pronounce correctly the words that you have studied this year, you are to review the words in Exercise 2, pages 17, 29, 76, 93, and in Exercise 3, pages 51 and 106. If you wish you may hold a contest. (See Exercise 2, page 63.)

II. The Use of Capitals and Marks of Punctuation

3. First give the rule for each capital and then copy the letter, putting in the marks of punctuation that are needed:

Lexington Mass
April 21 1775

Dear Abigail
    It was only two nights ago that we were roused by a call To arms to arms   Since then we have had a battle and sent the Red Coats back to Boston   At the sound of the call every able-bodied man hastily snatched his flintlock, and ran to the Common   I hope to be with the men again but I am now suffering from a wound

Your affectionate cousin
Ephraim Pillsbury

4. To make sure that you have written the letter

correctly, use the index at the end of this book to help you find the page on which the following directions occur: (1) Making a letter look neat, (2) Heading a letter, (3) Beginnings and endings for letters.

5. Study the directions, and then after re-reading the letter, re-write it, if necessary, to make it correct.

6. Think of a reason for each apostrophe:

> The officer's uniform was new.
> The soldiers' guns were left on the field.
> The general commanded, "Don't fire until the enemy reaches the fort."

7. Give the reason for each comma:

> The men carried flintlocks, powderhorns, and knapsacks.
> The commander shouted, "Stand!   The ground is your own, my braves!"
> "No, we are not to retreat until the powder is exhausted," said the soldier.

8. Copy these sentences, putting in the marks of punctuation that are needed:

> One day a friend of Paul Revere who lived in Boston came to see him   He came very quietly and secretly so as to escape the soldiers
> I have something to tell you he said   Some of the King's soldiers are going to Concord to get the powder that is there
> Indeed said Paul Revere   They shall get no powder if I can help it   When do they start
> At midnight the men rode through villages and towns and countryside   They knocked at doors and shouted Up   Up   Defend yourselves   The Redcoats are coming

9. If your paper is not satisfactory, find what

errors you have made and then review Exercises 4 and 5 on page 107. Later you are to do Exercise 8 again.

9. Writing for the Class Diary

[Written composition]

To complete your diary for the year you may wish first of all to write a report of your flag day entertainment and other interesting events in which your class has taken part. Decide upon your subject; write your report, read it over, and then give it to your teacher.

[Group story]

1. As a final group story for your class diary, be ready to write a description of your class as it is the last of the year. Read the description that you wrote the first of the year (see Exercise 1, page 21) and then decide what you would like to say. Keep in mind questions like the following: What changes have taken place in the class? What has the class enjoyed most during the year? In what has it improved most?

[Making a book]

2. After the group story has been copied and the other reports are all in, appoint a committee to bind the best reports for the year together as a magazine or book. Ask the committee to put the group stories and all others telling of school news in the first part of the book and the other fine stories and verses in the second part. Appoint some one to make out of heavy paper an attractive cover for the book.

3. When the book is finished, choose the stories that you would like to hear read.

[Writing a letter]

4. Before giving the book as a keepsake to your teacher, would it not be a pleasant thing to write her a letter telling her how much you have enjoyed the work at school this year and what experiences you remember best of all? She would appreciate it, too, if you were to thank her for all the help that she has given you.

10. Using Words Correctly. Review for the Second Half Year

Test D. Second Form. Speaking of One or More

Copy and complete, using *is* or *are:*

1. There ——— no clouds in the sky.
2. The days ——— growing warm.
3. The bluebird and the robin ——— here.
4. One of the birds ——— building a nest.

Copy and complete, using *was* or *were:*

5. When ——— the roses in bloom?
6. There never ——— any roses in the garden.
7. The bushes near the fence ——— killed by frost.
8. The pink rose and the yellow rose ——— blighted.

Read the first question in each exercise and then copy and complete the second question:

9. *Hasn't* Dick done his work? ——— the boys done their work?
10. *Aren't* we improving in our work? ——— I ——— improving in my work?
11. *Was* he at the meeting? ——— you at the meeting?
12. *Don't* they go to school? ——— she go to school?

Test E. Second Form. Words Often Confused

Copy and complete the sentences, using in each a word that sounds either exactly like the word printed in italics, or somewhat like it:

1. The box sent *to* us was —— large.
2. The seat in the boat was —— narrow *to* hold ——.
3. The boys laid *their* blankets on the ground and —— they slept.
4. In *our* room there —— forty children.
5. We all —— that we were to have *new* desks.

Test F. Second Form. Telling What Happened

Copy the second statement in each exercise, using a form of the word in italics to complete it:

1. The bell has *rung*. The bell ——.
2. School has *begun*. School —— at nine o'clock.
3. The children had *sung* a new song. The children —— a new song.
4. The books had *lain* on the shelf. The books —— on the shelf.
5. The plants had *sat* on the window-sill. Plants —— on the window-sill.
6. The class *drew* a map. The class had —— a map.
7. The castaways *drank* the last water in the flask. The castaways had —— the last water in the flask.
8. They had *eaten* all of the food. They —— all of the food.

A Fifth Grade Composition Score

In measuring a composition to find how good it is, try to answer the questions printed at the top of page 128; then compare it with the compositions that follow the questions.

Questions

Subject.   Is the subject something about which other boys and girls would like to hear?   Has enough thought been given to it?

Plan.   Does the composition form a connected story about one thing or is it a mere list of facts? Is enough said to make the point clear?   Does everything in the composition belong to the same story?

Interest.   Does the beginning help you to understand what follows?   Does the story grow more and more interesting as it proceeds?   Is the ending a good one?

Use of sentences.   Is the story told in separate and complete sentences?   Are the sentences clear in meaning?   Do they sound well?

Use of words.   Are all words correctly used?   Are they the best that could be chosen?

Note: All compositions in the following list should be marked *poor* unless they have some redeeming quality: (1) stories that sound mixed up or foolish; (2) long drawn-out accounts that have no point to them; (3) papers that are too brief to be clear; (4) stories that are told in "run-on" sentences; (5) compositions that contain many errors in spelling, capitalization, punctuation, or in the use of words.

This composition is *fair*.

A PICNIC

One day my cousins, my mother, and I went on a picnic.   We went to Parker River.   It was a very nice day.   We got there about ten o'clock.   Then we went in bathing.   When we came out of the water we had lunch.   After lunch we walked along the beach. We made tunnels in the sand and had great fun.   When we were going home the sun was setting and it was a very, very pretty sight.

Edwin

Edwin gives a clear idea of the picnic, but his paper would have been more interesting if, instead of giving a list of facts, he had told a story about building tunnels in the sand or about what happened when he was in bathing. His paper also fails to be really good owing to the fact that all his sentences except the last ones, are too abrupt to sound natural.

The following composition is *good*.

THE RESCUE

I have often been excited but never more so than one day last summer. My cousin and I were seeing which could walk out in the water the farthest. Another cousin of mine, who was three years old, said he could beat us, and he went out till we could not see him. Soon we saw him rising and sinking. He rose a third time. We were just in time to rescue him. We took him to land. Another time we knew enough to leave him at home.

Francis

In *The Rescue* Francis gives a clear idea of the excitement that he felt when he rescued his little cousin. Notice that the opening sentence prepares you for what is coming, and that all that is said forms a connected story about one incident.

The following compositions are *excellent*.

OUR PONY

One stormy night as I was putting "Dixie," our pony, to bed, there was all of a sudden a bright flash of lightning which scared her. She broke away from me and ran out into the field, a six-acre lot. I shut the upper and lower gates. Then there was a wild chase!

We tried oats, salt, sugar, hay, but everything failed
to attract her.   Finally after a lot of trouble we cor-
nered her in at the lower gate which was near the stable
and then our task was done.   We got her in and bolted
the door good and tight.

Charles

Notice that in Charles' composition the introduction helps you to understand what follows; the
story is told in a lively way; and the ending is good.

THE LOST HAT

It happened while we were on our way to Albany.
One very raw, cold morning when we were all bundled
up, a puff of wind blew my hat out of the machine.   My
brother stopped the machine and went out to get it.
But alas! a heavy truck had already gone over it.

What could I do?   Mother would not let me go
without a hat because of the weather.   While I was
wondering what to do, Daddy took out his newspaper
and began folding it.   I could not imagine what he
was doing.   I soon saw that he was making a hat for
me to wear.   Just as we got to the hotel, he put it on
my head.   Inside the hotel every one began laughing.
They all thought it was a big joke but I.

The next day mother bought me a beautiful new
hat and I was almost glad that it had happened.

Ruth

By telling her story well, Ruth has made what
might have been a dull story into an interesting one.
She has planned it carefully and told the story in
sentences that show variety; but the best feature
of her composition is her use of such telling expressions as "a *raw, cold,* morning," "a *puff* of
wind," "*But alas!*" "*a heavy* truck," "a *big* joke,"
"a *beautiful* new hat."

A Fifth Grade Program for Individual Progress in Form Study and Correct Usage

UNIT NO. 1

1. Using Words Correctly, page 5, Exercises 1, 2; page 6, Exercises 3, 4; page 7, Exercise 6; page 8, Exercise 8.

2. Practice in Using Other Words in Place of *And*, page 9, Exercises 3, 4; page 10, Exercises 7, 8; page 11, Exercises 9, 11.

3. Review Use of Capitals, page 13, Exercises 7, 8, 9.

4. Review, Punctuation, page 16, Exercises 8, 9; page 17, Exercise 10.

5. Capitals and Marks of Punctuation, page 18, Exercise 3.

6. The Sentence and Paragraph, page 18, Exercises 4, 5, 6; page 19, Exercise 7 (at top).

7. Using Words Correctly, page 19, Test A.

8. Practice Exercises for the Correction of Errors Made in Test A (if any). pages 263–268; Repetition of Test A, page 19.

UNIT NO. 2

1. Finding Sentence-Endings, page 23, Exercise 9.

2. Help in the Spelling of Words, page 23, Exercises 1, 2, 3, 4; page 24, Exercise 6.

3. Paragraphing a Letter, page 24, Exercises 2, 3, 4; page 25, Exercises 4, 7 c, 8.

4. Paragraphing a Conversation, page 28, Exercise 7; page 29, Exercise 8.

5. Using Words Meaning More than One, page 29, Exercise 3; page 30, Exercises 4, 5, 6.

6. Using Words Correctly, page 30, Test B.

7. Practice Exercises for Errors Made in Test B, see pages 268–270; Repetition of Test B.

UNIT NO. 3

1. Writing Titles of Books, page 34, Exercises 4, 5.

2. Titles in Sentences, page 39, Exercises 5, 6; page 40, Exercises 8, 9.

3. Writing a List of Books, page 50, Exercise 2.

4. Contractions, page 51, Exercises 4, 5, 6, 7, 8, 9.

5. Using an Index, page 51, Exercises 10, 11.

6. Using Words Correctly, Test C, page 52.

7. Practice Exercises for the Correction of Errors Made in Test C, pages 270–274; Repetition of Test C, page 52.

UNIT NO. 4

1. Abbreviations, page 63, Exercises 3, 4.

2. The Heading of a Letter, page 63, Exercise 5; page 64, Exercises 6, 7.

3. Three Kinds of Letters, page 64, Exercise 8; page 65, Exercise 9.

4. Using Words Correctly, page 66, Tests A, B, C.

BETTER EVERYDAY ENGLISH

PART TWO

BETTER EVERYDAY ENGLISH — PART TWO

Chapter I

IMPROVING OUR EVERYDAY SPEECH

1. Expressing Ideas Clearly

I

[Conversation and oral composition]

1. The boys and girls in the picture are enjoying a lively game of dodge ball. Perhaps you are unfamiliar with the game, but even so you may be able to tell something about it from the picture. Is it adapted to a large number of players or to a small number? Where is it played? What kind of ball is used? How are the players divided? Judging from its name, what do you think is the object of the game? Which team throws the ball? Which team tries to dodge it? What do you think happens to a player who fails to dodge a ball?

2. Dodge ball is played in two periods of a given number of minutes each. At the end of the first period the players left within the circle are counted as the score for those forming the inner team, and then the teams change places and the second half of the game is played. How do the players decide at the end of the game which team has won?

3. Which of the following games do you recognize?

The players form two companies. The members of one company fill their pockets with tiny scraps of paper. By scattering these scraps, they mark their trail as they run across fields, through the woods, and back to the starting-point or goal. Those in the other company try to capture the members of the first group before they reach the goal.

After choosing one person to be It and another person to run from him, the players form a double circle by standing two deep. The runner tries to get into a place in front of a row that is two deep, thus making the row three deep. If he can do this before he is caught by the one who is It, the person at the back of the row becomes the runner. If the runner is caught before he can get into place, he becomes It.

4. The games referred to in Exercises 1, 2, and 3 are adapted to a large group of players out of doors. What other games similar to these do you know?

5. What outdoor games do you know that are adapted to a small group of players?

6. Can you tell how to play a game and make your directions so clear that a person who is unfamiliar with the game will understand it?

7. With the help of the class tell how to play dodge ball.

8. Select a game that is one of your favorites. Without naming it, tell about the game in a way that will enable the boys and girls in your class to recognize it. Ask them to guess what you have in mind.

9. Compare these explanations. Which is easy to understand because it is told in clear sentences

and forms a connected story? What is wrong with the other explanation?

TEACHER

Teacher is a good outdoor game for from five to fifteen players. One person is chosen leader, or "teacher." The other players stand in line while the leader tosses a ball to each in turn. A player who fails to catch the ball goes to the foot of the line, or "class." If the leader misses the ball when it is returned to him, he, too, must go to the foot of the class. The one at the head then takes the leader's place.

DUCK ON THE ROCK

They try to get it off the rock before the leader catches them and every one has one throw, but if they can get it from the rock before they are caught they have another turn and the winner is the one who has the most ducks. You stand in a row and the one who is It stands near the rock, but he must not stand too near or he will get hurt.

10. In explaining a game, why should a person arrange his facts in order? Why should he avoid using words like *they* and *it* before he has mentioned that for which the words stand?

II

[Setting a high standard in English]

With your conversation and talks in mind, try to answer these questions:

1. What advantage has a boy (or girl) who can express his ideas clearly?
2. Why should every one set a high standard for himself in the use of English?
3. What habits should he cultivate?

2. A Better English Club

I. Forming a Club

1. One way in which the members of a class can help one another in their everyday speech is by forming a Better English Club.   Each month the club could hold meetings, plan posters, and work out other ways of improving the English of its members.

In forming such a club, a class should first of all discuss the kind of persons to choose for officers, and then, with the help of the following by-laws, make a set of its own.

BY–LAWS

Article I.   The club shall be called the Better English Club.

Article II.   The aim of the club shall be the improvement of the speech of its members at home, at school, on the playground, and elsewhere.

Article III.   The officers of the club shall be a president, a secretary, and a counselor.

Article IV.   It shall be the business of the president to call a meeting each month, and with the aid of the counselor to make a report of the progress made by the members of the club.   It shall be the duty of the secretary to keep a record of the errors made most frequently by the class.

Article V.   A poster committee shall be appointed by the club officers each month.   It shall be the business of this committee to make a Better Speech poster to be hung in the classroom.

Article VI.   The class teacher shall be invited to act as club counselor.

Article VII.   To become a member of the club, a person must promise to be on his guard against using poor English and to help others to avoid its use.   He shall keep this pledge in mind:

PLEDGE

I promise
> That I will try to use clear, correct English at all
> times.
> That I will pronounce my words distinctly, use a pleas-
> ant voice, and speak courteously.

II. Finding Out What Errors Need Correction

2. The following test covers some of the most common errors in the use of words.   It includes the errors allotted to the lower grades for self-correction and two new ones (see Questions 11 and 12) allotted to Grade Six.

Test G.   First Form.   Twelve Common Errors [1]

Copy the sentences, completing them with words from the list below Number 4:

1. On their voyage north the men ——— an iceberg.
2. The ship ——— from the south.
3. The men ——— their work well.
4. After school the boy ——— home.

saw	came	done	run
seen	come	did	ran

[1] This test takes for granted that no one in the club uses a double subject such as *Mary, she,* or *my father, he,* and that no one says *ain't, hain't, his'n, her'n, hisself, this here, that there, busted* or *them things*.   The test takes for granted also that no one uses *says* for *said,* or *give* for *gave.*

Copy and complete, using words that make sense:

5. I cannot write. I ——— no pencil.
6. Have you my pencil? No, I ——— your pencil.

In copying the answers to the questions, use words from the list below Number 12:

7. When are you and your father going away? My father and ——— are going to-morrow.

8. Where were you and your mother yesterday? ——— and ——— were at home.

9. Whom did Mary and her brother visit? Mary and ——— visited their aunt.

10. Was it Ruth's brother who was late? No, it was not ———.

11. How tall is Helen's brother? He is taller than ———.

12. To whom was the package sent? It was sent to my brother and ———.

I	her	me	he	him	her	I
me	she	I	him	he	she	me

3. Those who make errors in the test should use the Practice Exercises beginning on page 281.

III. Planning Posters

4. After the test papers have been corrected, the club is to find out what errors were made most frequently by the class. Members may then plan poster designs covering the correct forms for the errors, and submit the designs to the poster committee. The committee is to choose the best design and have a large copy made to be hung in the classroom. Members may illustrate quotations similar to those on page 141; they may use one of the suggestions given in the footnote on page 264; or, better still,

they may illustrate an original rhyme or carry out some plan of their own.

3. Giving New Items

[Conversation]

1. Most wide-awake boys and girls are interested in the latest news. They like to know what is taking place in their own school and town and what events of importance are occurring in the outside world.

2. What topics similar to the following interest your class?

News of school entertainments
Football and baseball victories
Playground improvements
Stories of bravery

News of the President
News of Congress
Work of the Red Cross
Discoveries and inventions

3. Why are topics similar to those mentioned in Exercise 2 better to discuss than news of crime, such as murder or theft? Why are they better than stories of accidents?

[Recognizing a sentence]

4. In order to report a news item in good English, a person should, of course, be able to recognize a sentence. Which of the following groups of words make complete sense by themselves? Which make you think something more is to be said?

   1. Labor Day a parade
   2. Every afternoon the boys in our school practice football
   3. The girls' cooking class
   4. Any one holding a public library card
   5. Our class is reading an interesting book which tells
   6. The boys and girls in the sixth grade have made window boxes and filled them with plants
   7. When the seventh grade gives an entertainment

5. Think of a news item in which your class would be interested. Be ready to give it in a complete and interesting sentence.

[Avoiding "chain" sentences]

6. Notice that the following news items are expressed in separate sentences, each complete in itself. The ideas are not joined, or "chained" by such words as *and*, *so*, and *then* used where they are not needed.

   Last Saturday the Girl Scouts of Troop 7 went on a trip to Long Pond. They cooked their lunch over camp fires and then practiced signalling.
   John and William Smith have built a cabin in the woods near their home. They made the cabin of old lumber and then painted it.

7. Think of some interesting enterprise carried on by a boy or girl in your neighborhood or elsewhere. If it is not a secret, be ready to tell about it in two or three separate sentences.

4. Sending News to Friends

[Conversation]

1. If a letter similar to the following was received by your class, how should you answer it?

Honolulu, Sandwich Islands
September 10, 1927

Dear Boys and Girls,

When school closed last June, I did not think that by fall I should be so far away from all of you. The last of July my mother and I received a telegram from my father saying that his business called him to Honolulu and that we were to meet him in San Francisco, ready to spend the year in the Sandwich Islands.

We had a fine voyage and I like it here on the island, but of course I miss my old friends. Please write me all the news.

Your old friend,
John Robinson

[Writing a letter]

2. Perhaps you have some one in mind who would be particularly glad to hear from your class. Decide what this person would like to know about your school; then, as your teacher writes on the board for you, dictate a letter.

3. After you are satisfied with the letter and it has been erased, divide the class into two sections. In one section include those who would like to write letters of their own to the person chosen. In the other section include those who would like to make a copy of the group letter, improving it wherever they can.

4. Before writing, review the directions on page 294.

5. Review.   Capitalization and Punctuation

I. The Use of Capitals

1. What rules for capital letters should a person keep in mind in writing a letter like the one on page 143?

2. What rules are needed in writing a conversation similar to the following?

> Suddenly the little brother called out, "Oh, what a funny little hole!   It bubbles."
> "Hole!   Where?" said Hans.
> "Here in the bank," said the little brother.
> "It is a hole in the dike!" cried Hans.   "What shall we do?"

3. Write two sets of rules for the use of capitals. Include in one set at least four rules that are needed in writing a letter.   Include in the other at least three that are needed in writing a conversation.

II. Marks of Punctuation

4. With the help of the selection in Exercise 2 give four rules for punctuation that a person should keep in mind in writing a conversation.

5. What rules for the comma are used in writing a letter similar to the one on page 143?

6. Write seven rules for punctuation.

7. Practice writing the selection in Exercise 2 until you can write it correctly with your book closed. You will remember, of course, to start a new paragraph with each change of speaker.

8. Copy this selection from *Alice in Wonderland*, putting in the marks of punctuation that are needed:

LIVE FLOWERS

O Tiger-lily said Alice I wish you could talk

We can talk said the Tiger-lily   when there's anybody worth talking to

At length as the Tiger-lily only went on waving about Alice spoke again in a timid voice — almost a whisper   And can all the flowers talk

As well as you can said the Tiger-lily   and a great deal louder

Alice didn't like being criticised so she began asking questions   Aren't you sometimes frightened at being planted out here with nobody to take care of you

There's the tree in the middle said the Rose   What else is it good for

But what could it do if any danger came   Alice asked

It could bark   said the Rose

It says 'Bough-wough' cried a Daisy   that's why its branches are called boughs

6. Mastery of the Sentence. Test No. 1

Copy the groups of words that form complete sentences:

1. When winter came
2. Early in the fall
3. Birds leaving for the south
4. The wind blew hard
5. The apples in the orchard were ripe
6. Although she was in a hurry, she stopped to put her room in order
7. The leader himself received a wound in the heart which was thought at first to be mortal but which proved

Find the ends of the following sentences; then copy the exercises, putting in the capitals and periods that are needed:

8. September sees a great change in the crows their moulting is over they are in full feather again and proud of their handsome coats their health is again good and with it their tempers are improved.

9. There was a great battle at sea one could hear nothing but the roar of big guns the air was filled with black smoke the water was strewn with broken masts and pieces of timber which the cannon balls had knocked from the ships.

Copy the following sentences, inserting in each the marks of punctuation needed to make the thought clear:

10. Tom where shall we carry you asked the men

11. Oh replied Little Thumb place me on the brim of your hat

12. The letter was dated Tokio Japan May 12 1927

13. The visitors enjoyed the beautiful mountains · the waterfalls and the display of flowers

Make one sentence out of those in each of the following exercises. You may omit words and add others, but you must not change the thought.

14. From the distance came the roar of the rapids. A sound of falling water came too.

15. The mountain seemed near. It was really many miles away.

16. The waterfall was a high one. It came from a mountain stream.

17. All winter long the bear slept in a hollow log. From this log he came forth in the spring. He was cross and hungry.

Compare your record on the test with the following standards. If you are not satisfied with it, ask for help and then repeat the test.

Standard score: *Fair*, 9–10 correct exercises; *good*, 11–12 correct exercises; *excellent*, 13–17 correct exercises.

Chapter II

MAKING A TALK INTERESTING

1. Giving a Talk in Geography

I

[Learning to study]

1. Your success in geography, as you know, is largely dependent upon your ability to get the thought in a selection and later to express it in clear English.

2. Can you tell in a single short sentence what this paragraph is about?

In the midst of the luxuriant vegetation of the tropics, animal life is wonderfully varied and abundant. There are tapirs, monkeys, and jaguars; brilliantly colored birds, such as parrots, and humming birds; and millions of insects. Scorpions and centipedes abound, and ants in countless numbers, some in the ground, others in decayed vegetation. Serpents, some of them poisonous, are common in the forests; and in the rivers are fish and alligators, the latter being found as far north as Florida and Louisiana.

3. If you wished to prove that there are many animals of many different kinds in the tropics, what facts could you give? (Use your dictionary to help you find the meaning of any words in the paragraph above that are new to you.)

4. Complete:

The main idea of the paragraph in Exercise 2 is ————

The facts that illustrate it are (1) ———— (2) ———— (3) ———— (4) ———— (5) ————

5. Try in reading the following paragraph once to find the main point in it and the facts that illustrate it:

> The animals that once inhabited the broad temperate zone have most of them been destroyed, although some still live in the forest and mountain regions.   When America was first visited by Europeans, the woods abounded in deer, moose, caribou, wolves, and foxes. Beavers built dams across the streams, mink and otter fished in the waters, and bears roamed at will.   Among the birds, the eagle was common, and wild pigeons and turkeys were so abundant that they were one of the principal foods of the early settlers.

[Giving a paragraph talk]

6. Be ready to give one of the paragraphs in Exercise 2 or 6 as a talk, paying no attention to the exact words of the text.   *Give the ideas.   Do not merely repeat words.*

II

[Summary]

7. Select an interesting paragraph from your next geography lesson and, with the following directions in mind, prepare a talk:

Studying a Paragraph

In studying a paragraph, look for the main idea.
With the main idea in mind try to recall the facts that illustrate it.
In making a report, express the thought in your own language, but do not avoid using new words.

8. You will also find it helpful to cultivate the habit of getting the thought from the first reading

and then of verifying it by a second reading.   Read the paragraph, think it over, and then test your thought by re-reading the paragraph.

9. In what ways can you make the dictionary help you?

2. Giving a Talk in History

I

[Learning to study]

1. A great event in history is portrayed in the following paragraph.   Can you name the event?

The day broke, and the New World lay before them. Some distance away they saw an island, thickly covered with trees, with crowds of natives running up and down its shores.   At sunrise the small boats were lowered, and Columbus, bearing the royal standard of Castile, and Martin Pinzon and his brother, each bearing a flag with a green cross, were rowed to the shore to the sound of music.   Columbus first stepped on the beach, the others followed, and all knelt and kissed the ground with tears and with thanks to God.   Then Columbus rose, shook out the gorgeous red and gold flag of Spain, and drawing his sword, took possession of the island in the name of the crown of Castile, calling it San Salvador.

2. Without re-reading the paragraph, answer as many of these questions as possible:

What did Columbus and his men see at daybreak? At what time did Columbus go ashore?   Who went with him?   What did each carry?   Who was the first to step on the beach?   What did Columbus do to show his gratitude at finding land?   In what way did he take possession of the island for Spain?

3. Complete this outline:

The main event reported in the paragraph is ———
The events that form a part of the main event are
(1) ——— (2) ——— (3) ——— (4) ———

4. With the outline in mind, give in your own words a picture of what is described in the paragraph in Exercise 1.

II

[Talking in paragraphs]

5. When you were younger, you were often contented if in class you could answer a question in a clear sentence. From now on you should strive to stand before your class and give talks a paragraph or more in length.

6. At your first opportunity in studying a history lesson, see that you prepare at least one such talk to give. Select a paragraph, get the main idea in mind, try to recall the related ideas, re-read the paragraph, and then be ready to give the thought in your own words.

3. Telling a Story Entertainingly

I

1. The following story tells of a bad fright experienced by a girl on her first visit to a farm. Perhaps you have had either a similar fright or some other exciting experience and can tell the class about it. Read the story, study the points on the pages that follow, and then be ready to give a talk.

AN EXCITING MOMENT

Once when I was a very little girl I visited my uncle's farm. It was a new experience for me and I wished to see everything, so one morning bright and early I started out for the barnyard. It was here that my red hair got me into trouble.

When I had finished looking at the interesting animals and fowls, I started back to the house. In the barnyard there was a winding path up a steep hill, which I was busily climbing when suddenly I heard a noise like the sound of hoofs. I glanced behind me and what should I see but a fierce-looking reddish-brown animal with projecting horns. It had seen my red hair and was running toward me with a wild look in its eye. I hurried up the hill as I had never hurried before, but, to my horror, I stumbled and fell! On and on came the dreadful creature, but just as it was upon me, some one grabbed me, and I was saved! A moment later I should have been tossed by an angry bull.

Selecting a Subject

2. You have learned in other years that the talks and stories most interesting to listen to are those that are confined to a single topic or event.   You would rather, for example, have some one tell you a story like the one on page 151 than to have him try to tell you all that he did during his summer vacation.

3. Which topic in each of the following pairs is limited enough to make a good subject for a story?

> My Dog — The Scrape My Dog Got Me Into
> Fishing — Landing a Big Fish
> Rescuing a Nestling — Studying Birds
> Taming a Squirrel — Squirrels
> An Automobile Trip — Losing Our Way
> A Boy Scout Hike — An Adventure in the Woods
> Boating — A Narrow Escape
> A Hallowe'en Adventure — Hallowe'en Fun

4. Name other topics that are limited enough to make interesting subjects.

Planning a Story

5. Compare the story on page 151 with the one given here.   Which forms a connected story about one event?   Which is a mere list of facts?

A VISIT ON A FARM

Once I went for a visit on a farm.   I visited the barnyard.   I saw cows and horses and pigs and chickens.   I had a ride on a hay wagon.   I drove the cows to pasture.   I played in a brook.   I went wading.   I played in the hay mow.   I climbed the trees in the orchard.

6. Tell what is wrong with this story:

POOR BOBBIE

Bobbie was my aunt's dog.   When we went to the country, we took him with us in our automobile.   We had a good time with him, but the dog had a bad end. When we got to Lowell, my aunt and I got out of the automobile to do some shopping and the dog got out too.   He saw another dog and ran after it.   That was the last we ever saw of poor Bobbie.

When we got to Mount Sunapee, we found a pretty little bungalow ready for us.   It was situated on Spectacle Lake.   Nearly every day we went bathing, fishing, and boating.   My brother spent the summer at a boys' camp.

7. What rules can you make for yourself in planning a story?

Holding the Attention of an Audience

[Choosing a good beginning].

8. To attract the attention of an audience, a speaker may choose a beginning that arouses curiosity or in some way gives an inkling of what he is going to say.

9. Think of other beginnings like the following:

About the worst mischief that I was ever in occurred when I was five years old.

I shall never forget my last birthday.

I have had many exciting experiences, but none so exciting as ———

The cellar was dark.   From a barrel in the corner I heard a sound of scratching.

One evening when I opened the barn door I saw two glaring eyes.

Last summer I visited ———.   What interested me most was ———

[Telling enough to make a point clear]

10. In order to make an impression on an audience, a person must tell enough about his topic to make his point clear.   If, for example, he is telling about landing a fish, he may tell how he knew the fish was on his line, the excitement he felt, how he played his line again and again and thus wore the fish out, and then how, with a sudden jerk, he landed the fish.

11. If you were telling about an experience in a dark cellar or basement, what details could you give to show that you were frightened?

12. Think of details that might be given in completing one of the following exercises:

    a. I had a difficult time making ———
    b. Some friends and I were once lost in the woods.
    c. One day when I was camping near a lake I had one piece of ill-luck after another.

[Choosing a good ending]

13. To leave an audience satisfied, a speaker should choose an ending that brings his talk to a definite conclusion.

14. Think of ways of ending stories about the following subjects:

    A search for a lost child
    Earning money with which to buy a puppy
    Building a Boy Scout shelter in the woods
    Winning enough honors to become an Eagle Scout

Making Sentences Sound Well

15. The sentences used in telling a story should be clear in meaning and should sound well.   Compare those in the story on page 151 with those in the story on page 152.   Which show variety in form and in length and for that reason seem full of life? Which sound monotonous and dull?

Choice of Words

[Choosing graphic words]

16. The words chosen in telling a story not only should be correct, but should exactly fit the ideas the speaker wishes to express, and thus help to make a story seem real.

17. Find the picture-making words in the following sentences:

The airplane glided to the surface of the water like a bird.

Oh, what a frightened feeling I had going down the long slide and landing in utter darkness!

[Avoiding unpleasant repetitions]

18. In the story of Poor Bobbie on page 153 there is an unpleasant repetition of the word *got*.   Tell how it could have been avoided.

19. Think of words that can be used in place of *got* in the following sentences:

1. I *got* a book from a shelf.   2. Henry *got* a bicycle for a birthday present.   3. Tom *got* a pair of skates at the store.   4. Ruth *got* permission to leave school at three o'clock.   5. Helen *got* home early.

20. The following words are some of those that

may be used in place of *said* in reporting a conversation.   What others can you add to the list?

asked   replied   remarked   exclaimed   cried   shouted

21. Why does a person need to know how to use a great many words?

Summary

22. With the points made on pages 152–155 in mind, write a set of rules to help you in story-telling. What kind of subject will you select?   What will you be careful to do in planning a story?   How will you secure and hold the attention of your listeners? What will you do to make your sentences sound well?   What care will you take in your choice of words?

II

[Telling stories]

23. Tell the story that you have been planning (see Exercise 1, page 150).   Try to keep in mind the five points given in your summary.

24. Be ready from day to day to volunteer other interesting stories telling of your own experiences. Think them out carefully and, if it is possible, rehearse them to some one.

4. Making a Collection of Stories

[Written composition]

1. In order to have a record of your work, plan to make a collection of your best stories so that you can bind them together at the end of the year.

2. For the first paper to put into your collection, write the story that you gave in your last lesson. Choose a brief but attractive title; then with the direction on page 290 in mind make a neat copy.

3. When you have finished your story, read it over to make sure that it contains no errors. Keep in mind the following questions: Is the story told in separate and complete sentences? Is the right mark of punctuation put at the end of each? Are capitals used where they are needed? Is the spelling correct?

4. When you are satisfied with your paper, you are to measure it by using the score on page 295.

5. Review and Practice

I. The Pronunciation of Words

1. The following words are frequently mispronounced. Can you pronounce all of them correctly? The words in parentheses will tell you what to watch for.

(Initial sound)	*(Mistaken sound)*	*(Final sound)*	*(Slighted syllable)*
what	across	kept	geography
why	have to	slept	arithmetic
which	often	just	poem
throw	drowned	reading	believe
that	attacked	writing	February
those	wrestle	going	library

2. To help the Better English Club in its work, hand to the president a list of the words that you hear frequently mispronounced on the playground and elsewhere.

II. Proof-Reading. The Comma

4. Give the rule for each comma:

   1. The sun had risen, but the air felt chilly.
   2. The address on Helen's letter was 5817 Madison Ave., Chicago, Ill.
   3. The letter was dated Tuesday, December 24, 1928.
   4. The postman brought a letter, a postal card, and a newspaper.
   5. The stranger said, "Boys, will you direct me to the railway station, please?"

5. Review the rules on page 293; then copy these sentences, putting in the marks of punctuation that are needed:

   1. The three boats in the fleet used by Columbus were the Santa Maria the Pinta and the Nina
   2. Friday morning August 3 1492 the little fleet sailed out of the port of Palos
   3. When the last island faded from sight the sailors wept like children
   4. Later on as they entered the belt of trade winds the men cried We are lost We shall never see our friends again

6. Proof-read your paper to make sure that you have used commas where they are needed.

6. A Sixth-Grade Newspaper

[Conversation]

1. Boys and girls in some sixth grades manage school papers. Such a paper need not be elaborate. It may be merely a collection of news items, jokes, poems, and stories written neatly and posted on a bulletin board or bound together in the form of a little magazine.

SCHOOL NEWS — FALL NUMBER

VOLUME I   SEPTEMBER   OCTOBER   NOVEMBER   NUMBER I

STAFF

Henry Parker . . . . . . Editor-in-Chief
Marion Evans . . . . . Assistant Editor
Gilbert Ryan . . . . Business Manager

EDITORIAL

The first of the school year is a good time to begin reading the right kind of books. We should broaden our minds by reading history, books about science, and good stories. To confine our reading, as many of us do, to exciting stories makes our minds like sieves. Nothing stays in them.

SCHOOL NEWS

To improve the appearance of their classroom, the boys and girls in the seventh grade have made their room into a city which they call Spotless Town. The desks are the homes which the citizens try to keep in perfect order. The teacher acts as mayor. Some members of the class belong to the Street Department; others belong to the Board of Health or to some other department. Every one holds an office of some kind.

The fat children, the slim children, the tall children, and the short children of the Edison are having a race with the children of the Washington School to see in which school the most children first reach the right weight for their height. Every one has joined the race and is trying to be a modern health crusader. All are keeping in mind that cleanliness, good food, fresh air, exercise, and plenty of sleep will help them in winning the race.

BOOK NOTICES

Stories of Four Pioneers is a book of thrilling stories telling the adventures of Daniel Boone, Kit Carson, Davy Crockett, and George Rogers Clarke. The book gives a good idea of pioneer days in Kentucky, Tennessee, and Missouri.

In the *Biography of a Grizzly* Thompson-Seton gives the life history of Wahb, a bear cub whose mother was shot. The story, which is a sad one, pictures wild life in the mountains of Idaho and in the Yellowstone Park.

Golden Numbers contains poetry on subjects of interest to boys and girls. As its name suggests, it is a book of value to all.

FUNNY STORIES

"Johnny, can you name a cape in Alaska?" asked a country school teacher.

"No'm," replied Johnny.

"Nome; that is right," commented the teacher. "Now, the next boy may name another."

"Have you lived here all your life?" asked a friend of five-year-old Dick.

"Not yet," answered Dick.

2. Be ready to give other ideas as to how a school paper may be published, and then to express your opinion on the following points:

    1. The kind of person to choose as the editor-in-chief; as an assistant editor; as a business manager.

    2. The desirability of having contributions from every member of the class published often during the year.

    3. The advantage of having all contributions written on paper of uniform size.

    4. The necessity of having all papers free from errors in spelling, capitalization, punctuation, and the use of words.

                               [Written composition]

3. Write a news item, a nature observation, a book notice, a good joke, or an interesting story that might be used in a school paper.

4. Explain the use of capitals and marks of punctuation in the two funny stories in the *School News* and then proof-read your own paper to make sure that it is correct.

7. The Use of Names

I. Surnames

1. Each of us has at least two names, the name given to us when we were born and a last name, or surname. A long time ago, when there were only a few people living in a group, the people had no surnames. They were called by given names, such as John and Mary. When there were too many Johns and Marys, surnames came into use. These surnames were sometimes taken from the trade a man followed, sometimes from a place, and sometimes

from a nickname. John, the carpenter, came to be called John Carpenter; John, of the town of Wakefield, came to be called John Wakefield; and John, the red-headed, came to be called John Reade (*Reade* meant *red-headed*).

2. Tell, if you can, the origin of each of the following surnames:

Smith	Strong	Whitehead
Baker	Miller	Atwood
Little	Townsend	Johnson

3. Try to find out from your father the origin of your own surname. Ask from what country it came and what it meant originally.

4. Try also to find the origin of the name of your town and state.

II. Nouns

5. Besides being referred to by a particular name, a person is sometimes spoken of as a man, a woman, a boy, a girl, or a child. In the same way a place may be called by its name or it may be spoken of as a town, city, or village. All these words are names.

6. Notice the names in italics:

Lincoln was born in a log *cabin* in *Kentucky.*

Such words as *Lincoln, cabin,* and *Kentucky* are **nouns.**

A noun is the name of a person, place, or thing.

7. Give at least three nouns that name:

1. Objects in nature. Begin with *rock.*

2. Pieces of furniture. Begin with *chair*.
3. Trades. Begin with *weaving*.
4. Kinds of animals. Begin with *bear*.
5. Kinds of birds. Begin with *oriole*.
6. Traits of character. Begin with *honesty*.

III. Common and Proper Nouns

8. Notice the difference in the nouns in these two sentences:

a. The girl spent a holiday in the city.
b. Marion spent Christmas in New York.

9. Names like *girl*, *city*, or *holiday* may be applied to a large class of objects. When we say *girl*, we may mean any girl; when we say *city*, we may mean any one of a number of cities; and, when we say holiday, we may mean any one of several holidays.

Names like *girl*, *city*, and *holiday* that may be applied to any one of several objects in a class are called **common nouns**.

10. Names like *Marion*, *New York*, and *Christmas* refer to particular persons, places, and things. When we say *Marion*, we usually mean a particular girl; when we say *New York*, we mean a particular city; and, when we say *Christmas*, we mean a particular holiday.

Names like *Marion*, *New York*, and *Christmas* referring to particular persons, places, and things are called **proper nouns**.

A common noun is a name that may be applied to any object of its kind.

A proper noun is the name of a particular person, place, or thing.

11. Give a common noun naming something that can be seen on a farm; at a circus; in a kitchen; in a grocery.

12. Give a proper noun used as a name for a boy; for a girl; for a city; for a state; for a country.

13. Name a common noun showing to what or whom each of these proper names may be applied. Example: Rover, dog.

Rover	Mrs. Smith	Illinois	Atlantic
Tabby	Dr. Jones	Mississippi	America
Starface	Mary	Erie	New Year's Day
Dobbin	Henry	Boston	Pike's Peak

A proper noun should begin with a capital letter.

14. Which of these nouns are proper names? Which should always begin with a capital letter?

John	Washington	Chicago	Mountain
Children	Dogs	Lake	River
City	Ocean	Missouri	Canada
Pacific	Mary	Elm Street	Cuba

15. Point out the proper nouns in the letter on page 143.

16. Make a list of ten common nouns and of ten proper nouns.

IV. Review.   Plurals and Possessives

17. Write the plural for each of these nouns:

turkey	knife	potato	woman
bush	half	mouse	child
fox	lady	man	ox

18. Copy these sentences, filling the blanks with the possessive form of the nouns given below Number 5:

1. The ——— hat was lost.
2. The ——— collar was new.
3. The ——— rattle was broken.
4. The ——— horse was strong.
5. ——— uncle took him for a ride.

    boy   dog   baby   man   Tom

19. Change each possessive noun to plural form:

1. The boy's playground was large.
2. The girl's lessons were hard.
3. The soldier's tent was new.
4. The farmer's barns were burned.
5. The carpenter's tools were lost.

8. Using Words Correctly

Test H.   First Form.   Giving Words their Right Meaning

Copy and complete, using words from the list given below Number 6:

1. May I ——— a pencil from you?
2. The work was ——— finished.
3. The pitiful old man looked ———.
4. John's father ——— him how to swim.
5. The weather was ——— pleasant.
6. The dress was ——— on the chair.

borrow   almost   funny   taught   real   laying
lend   most   strange learned   very   lying

Those who make errors in the test should use the Practice Exercises beginning on page 282.

For poster suggestions, see Exercise 4, page 140.

Chapter III — OLD DAYS AND NEW

1. Ways of Helping the Class

[Conversation]

1. The people living a hundred years ago, as we all know, had few of the comforts and the advantages that we have nowadays. The houses were poorly heated, cooking was done over an open fire and the food was plain; clothes were made by hand from homespun cloth, journeys were made by stage-coach or on horseback; books and newspapers were rare, and most of the schools were little one-room buildings, poorly equipped.

2. This chapter will help you to contrast our present advantages with those of olden times. It will also enable you to look up facts about the history of your own town. In planning how you can be of assistance in the work, be ready to talk over some of the following questions:

Where can we find pictures that will help us in this study?

What stories give a good idea of a hundred years ago?

How can we find out interesting facts about the history of our town?

[Written composition]

3. Try to think of old residents in your town who might be willing to tell you stories of earlier days. With these people in mind, perhaps your class will

find it possible to send out letters of request similar to the one given here:

A LETTER OF REQUEST [1]

———— School, ————, ————
November ————, ————

My dear Mr. ————,

Our class is trying to learn something about other days in our town. If we are not asking too much of a busy person, we should like to have you write us a letter telling us a story of your own boyhood days.

Sincerely yours,
The Sixth Grade

4. The following letter of acknowledgment may help you later in planning one of your own:

A LETTER OF ACKNOWLEDGMENT

———— School, ————, ————
November ————, ————

My dear Mr. ————,

Your interesting letter was read to our class to-day. We all enjoyed listening to it, particularly the part telling of what you did at school. We thank you very much for taking the time to write us.

Sincerely yours,
The Sixth Grade

2. Going to School

[Conversation]

1. In the school of a hundred and more years ago, the children studied a little spelling and geography and the so-called three R's — reading, 'riting, and 'rithmetic. They had no gymnastics, no manual train-

---

[1] This letter may be one requesting an old settler to talk to the class.

ing and no cooking, and were taught no music, no drawing, and no nature study or science. The teacher was very severe. If a pupil made a mistake or was mischievous, the teacher sometimes put him on a dunce stool and sometimes punished him with a birch rod or with a whip. The people in those days thought that "to spare the rod spoiled the child."

2. The picture on page 169 shows a schoolmaster conducting a spelling lesson with Jonathan, Abigail, and Obadiah in his class. What do you think will happen if Jonathan misspells a word? How will this affect little Abigail and the other children, — Betty who is doing her sums with a creaking slate pencil, naughty Amos who is about to take a bite of an apple, and poor little Ezekiel sitting on the dunce stool?

3. What do you notice about the schoolroom shown in the picture? How does it differ from your own?

[Using an outline]

4. Give in turn with other members of the class the facts called for in the first part of the following outline, and then supply what is missing in the second part:

Our Schoolroom Compared with One of Olden Times

I. A schoolroom of olden times: the barrenness of the walls; the wooden benches used for seats; the small number of books and maps; the poor lighting and heating.

II. Our schoolroom: ———; ———; ———; ———; ———.

5. Tell how to complete this outline and then give the facts called for in both sections:

Attending School

I. Attending a school in olden times: the three R's; the severity of punishments for slight offences; the lack of opportunity for the pupils to show self-control.

II. Attending a modern school: ———; ———; ———.

[Giving talks]

6. Use one of these suggestions:

a. Pretend that you are one of the pupils shown in the picture. Give yourself an old-fashioned name and then tell the class about your school.

b. With the help of the outline in Exercise 4 or the one in Exercise 5 give a talk comparing your school with one in olden days.

c. Get from your grandparents or some one else a story of the school which they attended. Make a report to the class.

d. Make up a sad story about little Ezekiel; or tell a funny incident that might have happened in an old-fashioned school.

7. Why, before giving your talk, should you have an outline of it well in mind and know just what you will say on each topic?

II

[Vocabulary study — Nouns]

8. What old-fashioned names were given to the children mentioned in Exercise 2? These are Bible names. What others like them have you heard?

9. What are some of the things that you would

find in an old-fashioned school that you would not find in your own school?

10. Complete each list, naming other nouns:

Articles found in an old-fashioned school: dunce-stool, ———

Articles found in a modern school: pictures, ———

11. Which nouns in Exercise 2 on page 167 are proper nouns? How can you tell which they are?

12. Write a brief description of the scene pictured on page 169. Bring into it the names of the children.

13. Proof-read your paper (see Exercise 12) to make sure that you have spelled each word correctly and used capitals for all proper nouns.

14. Complete Exercise 10 in writing; then make a list of twelve or more proper nouns that you use frequently.

3. Travel

I

[Conversation]

1. Before the days of railroads, journeys overland were largely made by stagecoach. Long before the Revolutionary War stage roads were built from Boston to Albany and from New York to Philadelphia. The stagecoach, which was drawn by from four to eight horses, ran on these roads at regular times; at first, weekly; and later, daily. Along the route at intervals were inns where the drivers changed horses and where passengers alighted for refreshments.

2. Tell what you think were some of the difficulties of stagecoach travel.

[Learning to study]

3. Fast railway trains now carry thousands of passengers daily from Boston to New York. The journey takes a little over five hours. The following paragraph will show you how different travel was in olden days:

FROM BOSTON TO NEW YORK BY STAGECOACH

At the time of our Revolution two stagecoaches were enough for all passengers between Boston and New York. The journey began at three o'clock in the morning. Horses were changed every twenty miles, and, if the roads were in good condition, some forty miles would be made by ten o'clock in the evening. In bad weather, when the passengers had to get down and lift the clumsy wheels out of deep ruts, the progress was much slower. Broad rivers like the Connecticut and the Housatonic had no bridges. To drive across them in winter, when they were solidly frozen over, was easy; and in pleasant summer weather to cross in a row boat was not a dangerous undertaking. But squalls in some seasons and floating ice in others were things to be feared. After a week or ten days of discomfort and danger the jolted and jaded travelers reached New York.

JOHN FISKE, *Adapted*

4. With the help of others in the class give in turn the facts called for under the first topic of the following outline; then tell what might be included under the second topic:

Old Times and New in Travel

I. Travel in olden days between New York and Boston: means used; the number of people carried; time required; discomforts and delays experienced; dangers encountered.

II. Travel in modern days between New York and Boston: ——; ——; ——; ——; ——.

5. Which of the following comparisons interests you the most?   How would you outline a talk in which you made the comparison?

Crossing the plains in a prairie schooner, or covered wagon, compared with a similar journey by automobile.

The first automobiles compared with those used nowadays.

Travel by airplane or airship compared with travel by railway or steamship.

A journey taken by your great-grandfather compared with one taken by your father.

6. Suggest other comparisons that might be made in a talk on old and new ways of travel.

7. Use one of the following plans or a plan suggested in Exercise 5 or 6:

a. Pretend that you have taken the trip by stagecoach from Boston to New York.   Tell the story of your trip.

b. With the help of the outline in Exercise 4, give a talk showing the advantages of travel by railway over that by stagecoach.

c. Tell a true story of a journey or voyage taken by your grandfather or grandmother.

d. Describe two scenes, one of old-time travel and one of modern days.   Let the class name them.

e. Make up a story telling of an adventure in a stagecoach, in a prairie schooner, or in an airplane. Have it exciting, but tell only what could really happen.

8. Select your subject carefully so that your talk will not only be interesting, but will also in some way differ from the talks given by others in the class. Write in outline form the main topics for your talk or story; show the topics to your teacher for her approval; then rehearse your talk.

II

[Vocabulary study — Nouns]

9. Find how long a list you can make of nouns (1) that name things connected with stagecoach travel; (2) that name things connected with an automobile.

10. Which nouns in the selection on page 171 are proper nouns?

11. Make sure that you can spell all the words used in the selection; then, with your book closed, write from memory as much of the story as you can.

12. In proof-reading your paper, pay particular attention to your manner of writing the proper nouns.

4. The Story of a Pioneer

[Learning to study]

1. The men who explored the west and those who settled it were men of sturdy character, quick of mind, and brave of heart. Among the pathfinders none was more daring than Christopher Carson, or, as he is often called, Kit Carson. The following story shows the kind of adventures he sometimes met.

AN ENCOUNTER WITH BEARS

One afternoon, having traveled for hours through a very dreary and barren ravine, Carson came upon a herd of elk. Moving with great care circuitously, he entered upon a covert of trees and fired a shot at the largest of the herd. The animal stood for a moment and then dropped dead.

Carson was more than usually elated by his success, but scarcely had the echo of his rifle shot died away when he heard a terrific roar directly behind him. Instantly turning his head, he saw two enormous grizzly bears only a few rods away coming down upon him at full speed.

He had discharged his rifle, and for once Kit Carson was frightened; but not so much as in the slightest degree to lose his self-possession. With a lightning glance his eye swept the grove in search of a tree into whose branches he might climb. He saw one at a little distance, and rushed toward it, pursued by both the monsters, growling and gnashing their teeth. With wonderful agility Carson sprang and caught a lower branch and drew himself up into the tree just in time to escape the blow which one of the bears struck at him with his terrific claws.

[Keeping a story moving]

2. The story of Kit Carson is like a moving pic-

ture. Something is happening all the time and the story becomes more and more exciting as it goes along. Name the chief event in each paragraph, and then tell where in the story the most thrilling moment occurs.

3. Judging from its use in the story, what should you say was the meaning of each of the words given here in italics?

barren ravine   *elated* by his success
moving *circuitously*   *enormous* grizzlies
a *covert* of trees   springing with *agility*

4. Use a dictionary to help you in making sure that you have given the correct meaning to each word.

5. A bear has a tender nose. Kit Carson had with him a sharp knife with which he whittled a stick. With these facts in mind mention some of the things that might be used to make the story of Kit Carson's escape from the bears a lively one.

6. Be ready with a suggestion for a thrilling story telling of an adventure similar to Kit Carson's. The story may be about meeting a wild animal or it may be about Indians.

[Written composition]

7. Choose b or c, if possible; otherwise choose a:

a. Pretend that you are Kit Carson. With your book closed write a thrilling story of the adventure given in Exercise 2.

b. Write a story showing how Kit Carson may have escaped from the bears.

c. Write either an original story of adventure, or one that you have read about Daniel Boone or some other pioneer.

8. Before reading your paper to the class, look it through to make sure that you have made it as interesting as possible.

9. Proof-read your paper with the suggestions on page 292 in mind.

5. Stories from Local History

[Planning a program]

1. In carrying out the program for the story hour planned on page 165, be ready to do one of the following things: (1) to repeat a story about early days told you by your grandparents; (2) to read a reply that the class received from a letter sent to an old resident; (3) to show a picture of early days in your town; (4) to report on the first fire department, the first railway, the first school, the first church, or on some other similar topic.

2. The following story is one of several that a sixth-grade class in the State of Washington obtained from early settlers. It will give you an idea of the kind of incidents your class will enjoy hearing about.

TROUBLE WITH AN INDIAN CHIEF

Moses was an Indian chief who at one time went on the warpath against the white people. His warriors killed two of the settlers. Moses was captured and some of the people wanted to have him killed, but others thought it wiser to use a different plan. They decided to take him to Washington and show him the

President. When he returned home, he was very proud. He said he would never bother the white people again, and he was as good as his word, for he gave them no more trouble.

3. Before planning a talk, review the summary on page 289. What use can you make of an outline?

6. Review and Summary

I. Pronunciation and Meaning of Words

1. The words printed in italics in the following sentences are ones that you have used in this chapter. Show (1) that you can pronounce each correctly and (2) that you can use it in a sentence of your own:

> 1. The school children in olden times were often *mischievous*.
> Travelers by stagecoach *encountered* many dangers.
> Carson entered a barren *ravine*.
> By climbing a tree with *agility*, Carson escaped the bears.
> The grizzlies were *enormous*.

2. Write your sentences, being careful to spell all words correctly.

II. Talking in Sentences

3. Be ready to play this game:

Historical Riddles

The class forms two teams. Each member of a team must choose an historical event with which the class is familiar and relate it in three or four separate and complete sentences. If he is successful in composing a riddle that is interesting but hard for the other team to guess, he scores a point for his side. The riddles given may be similar to the following.

A ship loaded with a cargo of tea was anchored in a harbor. A band of men, dressed as Indians, stole out in the dead of night, rowed to the ship, and boarded it. After giving many war whoops and brandishing their tomahawks, the men threw the tea overboard.

If a topic chosen by a player is used by some one else before he has a chance to give his riddle, he must immediately choose a new topic.

III. Proof-Reading.   Paragraphing

4. Find in this story where a new topic starts and then copy the story, writing it in two paragraphs:

PUTTING OUT A FIRE

In olden days men put out a fire with water carried in fire buckets.

When a fire alarm was given, each citizen seized his fire bucket and ran to the fire.

The men formed two lines, called the dry lane and the wet lane, leading to and from a well.

At the well a man filled the buckets and sent them up the wet lane.

As soon as a bucket was emptied, it was sent down the dry lane to be filled again.

Nowadays men use engines and hose.

At the sound of the alarm, fire apparatus goes speedily to the fire.

Firemen quickly attach the hose to a hydrant.

A powerful engine forces a stream of water on the fire.

IV. Preparing a Paper to Keep

5. Decide which of the talks that you prepared in the lessons beginning on pages 166, 170, 173, and 176, you would like to have in written form so that you can bind it with other papers that you are planning to keep. With an outline in mind determine how many paragraphs the talk requires and then write your paper. Before giving it to your teacher to keep, proof-read it for spelling, sentence endings, capitalization, and punctuation.

7. Words Needed in Stating a Fact

I

[Words expressing action]

1. In expressing our thoughts, we need first of all the names of persons and things and then words expressing action. We say, for example, "*Men plow*," "*Women sew*," "*Children play*." In these sentences the words *men*, *women*, and *children* are names of persons, and are called **nouns**; the words *plow*, *sew*, and *play* tell us of actions made by the persons. Such words are called **verbs**.

2. In speaking of the actions of a hunter with a gun, we might use the verbs *load*, *aim*, *shoot*. Give verbs that tell what is done:

1. By farmers. Begin with *plow*.
2. By carpenters. Begin with *saw*.
3. By housekeepers. Begin with *sweep*.
4. By boys playing games. Begin with *toss*.
5. By girls in doing fancy work. Begin with *crochet*.
6. By children at school. Begin with *study*.
7. By dogs. Begin with *bark*.

3. Supply verbs expressing action:

1. In olden times women ——— yarn.
2. They ——— their own cloth.
3. They ——— stockings for their children.
4. They ——— clothes.
5. They ——— long seams by hand.
6. The farmer's cattle ——— their grain.
7. The horses ——— when they saw the man.
8. The sheep ——— together in fright.
9. The oxen ——— the heavy logs.
10. The dog ——— slowly after his master.

4. Find in each sentence the word showing action:

11. The pioneer built a log cabin in the woods.
12. He chopped down trees.
13. He fitted the logs together.
14. He plastered the cracks with mud.
15. Herds of buffalo fed on the prairie.
16. Deer hid in the woods.
17. Otter swam in the ponds and rivers.

5. Find in the story of Kit Carson and the bears at least twenty verbs showing action. Make a list of them.

II

[Verbs expressing conditions]

6. In the exercises in Section I the verbs express action. Other ideas may be expressed by a verb. We may say, for example, that *Fire is hot* or *The days are long*.

7. The words *is* and *are* are used in telling the state or condition of a person or thing. These are verbs of *being*.

8. Since a verb is used in telling a fact either by expressing action or by giving the state or condition of its subject, we may say that a verb is a "telling word," or we may use this definition:

A verb is a word used to assert action or being.

9. In these sentences the verbs express ideas that are associated with the five senses. Tell to which sense each corresponds.

The mountain *looks* high.   The noise *sounded* strange.
The lilies *smell* sweet.   Fur *feels* soft.
Vinegar *tastes* sour.

10. Supply verbs giving the state or condition of the person or thing named. Use a different word in each sentence.

Iron ——— heavy.   The child ——— pale.
Feathers ——— light.   The echo ——— faint.
The traveler ——— tired.   The flowers ——— sweet.
The water ——— salt.   The air ——— cold.

III

[Verb phrases]

11. Sometimes two or three words are used as a verb. Notice the verbs in italics in these sentences:

1. The farmer *was plowing*.
2. The farmer's wife *had been churning*.
3. Father *is going* on a trip.
4. Mother *can bake* good cookies.
5. The curfew *will ring* at nine o'clock.
6. By April the birds *will have returned*.

Was plowing, had been churning, is going, can bake, will ring, and *will have returned* are **verb phrases.**

12. Use these verb phrases and express in interesting sentences different ideas about travel:

is hurrying	can travel	should have stopped
were carrying	may start	might have warned
had been buying	will leave	could have gone
are sailing	has gone	should have arrived

8. Using Words Correctly

Test I. First Form. Telling What Happened

Read the first statement in each exercise and then copy the second statement completing it with a form of the word in italics:

1. The sun *rose* behind a cloud.   The sun had ———.
2. The travelers *went* north.   The travelers have ——— north.
3. The men *saw* a caravan.   The men had ——— a caravan.
4. The caravan *came* from across a desert.   The caravan had ——— from across the desert.
5. The men *chose* a leader.   The men had ——— a leader.
6. The caravan *took* the long route.   The caravan had ——— the long route.
7. The camels *lay* under the trees.   The camels had ——— under the trees.
8. The drivers *sat* beside them.   The drivers had ——— beside them.
9. The boys *wrote* a story.   The boys had ——— a story.
10. The artist *drew* a picture.   The artist had ——— a picture.

For Practice Exercises see pages 270–274.

Chapter IV—WRITING LETTERS

1. Three Secrets of Letter-Writing

[Conversation]

1. When the postman delivers a letter, we often hail it with delight, particularly when it is from a person who writes entertaining letters.

2. Think over some of the letters that you have been glad to receive. Try to discover the secret of their success.

3. In what ways can a person make his letters a tribute to his friends and a credit to himself?

4. What characteristics of a good letter are shown in the following?

> Pembroke, New Hampshire
> August 15, 1927

Dear Ben,

Here we are on Aunt Mary's farm enjoying ourselves. We have plenty of things to do, such as fishing in the river, going boating, riding horseback, hunting eggs, helping the men in the fields, and — eating apples!

Aunt Mary keeps bees and I have been watching them make honey, but never in the daytime, however, as they are apt to sting you if you go near them when they are at work. At dusk they do not mind being watched. Now is the bees' busiest time, for the buckwheat is in full bloom. The little white blossom of this grain contains a great deal of honey. When we pass the fields, we hear a continuous droning sound from the bees in the flowers.

We boys wish you were with us. How do you enjoy camp life? We hope to hear from you soon.

> As ever,
> Richard

[Planning letters]

5. Show that the boy who wrote the letter kept the following directions in mind and that therefore he knew three secrets of making a letter a success: (1) think of something to write that will interest the person to whom you are writing; (2) write as you talk; (3) keep on one topic long enough to say something interesting about it.

6. Why should a person avoid showing any evidence of haste or carelessness in his letters? Why should he never use figures or abbreviations except in writing the date or an address?

7. Name an interesting experience that you have had lately. Have you been on a trip? Have you attended a lecture, read an enjoyable book, or seen a good moving picture? Has something of unusual interest happened at home? Are you making anything?

[Writing letters]

8. Choose some relative or friend who would be glad to receive a letter from you. Decide what this person would like to hear about and then plan your letter.

9. Compose your letter carefully and make it look neat. See that in every way it is a tribute to the person to whom you are writing and a credit to yourself.

10. Read your letter with the directions on page 294 in mind.

11. Show on a slip of paper how you would address the envelope in which to enclose your letter.

William   Margaret

2. Meeting a Stranger at a Railway Station

[Making a description clear]

1. William's cousin has never seen him. Judging from his picture, what do you think could be said to the cousin to help him in picking out William in a crowd at a railway station? He is twelve years old. Is he large or small for his age? Is he fair or dark? How is he dressed? Is there anything noticeable about the way he stands or about the expression of his face?

2. What might be said of Margaret that would help a stranger to recognize her?

3. Show that you can give a clear description in playing *Who's Who*. Choose a member of your class. Without mentioning his name, give a description of him that would enable a stranger to recognize him in a crowd at a railway station. Ask your classmates to tell whom you have in mind. All descriptions must, of course, be courteous.

4. What is said in this letter to make the description clear?

244 Hennepin Avenue
Minneapolis, Minnesota
January 10, 1928

My dear Uncle Charles,

You were very kind to offer to meet me in Chicago and to help me cross the city. Since you have never seen me you will wish to know what kind of boy to look for. I am twelve years old, but tall for my age. My eyes are gray like my mother's, my hair is light, and I am freckled (just a little!). I think, however, that the best way for you to recognize me will be by my baggage. If you see a tall boy in a brown suit lugging a suit-case, an umbrella, a pair of snowshoes, and a big lunch basket, you will know that it is I!

Mother sends her love to you and asks me to thank you for your kindness.

Your affectionate nephew,
Robert Hutchinson

[Writing a letter]

5. Plan a letter to your teacher. Describe yourself so that a stranger could recognize you. Sign the letter with a fictitious name, and after getting a classmate to copy the letter for you, give it to your teacher. Find how many members of the class she can recognize from the descriptions given.

3. A Letter of Thanks

[Conversation]

1. A person who gives us a present usually takes time and thought in selecting it, and perhaps makes a personal sacrifice to obtain it for us. For this reason we should thank him promptly, and, by mentioning just what we admire about the gift, show how much pleasure it has given us. When the present is one for which we do not care, we can at least express our appreciation of the kindness of the giver.

2. Name a present that has given you pleasure. Tell what you think would have been appropriate to say in thanking the person who gave it to you.

[Written composition]

3. Pretend that a friend has given you a present for which you have longed. Write him (or her) a letter thanking him for it. Mention just what, in imagination, you admire about the gift and how much pleasure you expect to take in it.

4. Writing a Business Letter

I

[Conversation]

1. When you take up the work in Chapter VI, you will have an opportunity of forming a travel club. In order to obtain pictures and information, plan to write for booklets which railway companies and steamship lines distribute for the cost of the postage. Collect advertisements from different mag-

azines and decide which booklets will be of service to you.

2. A business letter should be neat in appearance, clearly and briefly expressed, and written without errors.

3. Tell how the following business letter differs from a friendly letter in its salutation and its close:

HEADING............214 South Pine St., Atlanta, Ga.
                                    Jan. 15, 1927
ADDRESS ...... ——— Railway,
                            St. Paul, Minn.
SALUTATION....Gentlemen:
                        You will find enclosed six cents
            in stamps.   Please send me the booklet
            on Yellowstone Park advertised in the
            December number of the National Geo-
            graphic Magazine.
COMPLIMENTARY CLOSE........Yours truly,
SIGNATURE......................Robert Mann

[Group composition]

4. Choose some one to write on the board for you and then dictate a request for the booklet men-tioned in the following advertisement:

Unique pleasures in a perfect summer vacation land. Send 6¢ in postage for booklet describing the Yosemite, the twin peaks, Mt. Lowe and Mt. Wilson, the San Fernando Valley, and the Spanish missions. Address ——— Railway Company, Los Angeles, California.

5. Divide your class into committees.   Each com-mittee, with the help of its chairman, is to select an advertisement of a booklet and write a letter similar to the one in Exercise 3.

II

6. Many people avoid the use of abbreviations in the heading and address of a friendly letter, but use them in a business letter when they are without the convenience of a typewriter and wish to save time and space.

7. In the letter on page 188 the abbreviation *Ga.* stands for *Georgia* and *Jan.* for *January.* What other abbreviations are used?

8. What words are often abbreviated in writing an address on an envelope?

9. For what words do these abbreviations stand?

Mr.	Rev.	Lieut.	St.	Mass.	Sept.
Mrs.	Hon.	Col.	Ave.	Wis.	Oct.
Dr.	M.D.	Gen.	Rd.	Tex.	Nov.

10. Notice that the following dates may be written in two ways:

January 3, 1927
Jan. 3, 1927

December 25, 1930
Dec. 25, 1930

February 14, 1928
Feb. 14, 1928

November 11, 1918
Nov. 11, 1918

11. Which five months have names so short that they are not usually abbreviated?

12. Write the heading of a letter, using abbreviations in the address and date.

13. Show on slips of paper how to address letters to different business firms in your town. See that all abbreviations that you use are correctly written.

14. Write on a slip of paper the address to be used on the envelope which is to enclose the letter written in Exercise 5.

[Proof-reading]

15. Proof-read your letter (see Exercise 5, page 188) for the use of abbreviations and for errors of all kinds.

16. Make a list of the abbreviations in Exercise 9 and the words for which they stand.

5. School News. Fun Number

1. Appoint, with your teacher's approval, three editors for the *Fun Number* of the *School News*. Choose one editor to take charge of the papers on games; a second editor for the jokes; and a third for the riddles and puzzles.

2. The editors are to explain to the class just what they would like to have contributed to the paper, and then every member is to submit at least one item that the editors asked for.

6. Writing a Notice

[Conversation]

1. Read this notice and the one on page 192; then tell what facts are given to make each of them clear:

The sixth and seventh grades of the Washington School will give a Verdi concert in the School Assembly Hall on June the first at four o'clock. There will be sixteen numbers. Some selections will be played on a victrola; the others will be given by the school orchestra. Admission, ten cents.

THE SCHOOL NEWS — FUN NUMBER

Volume I   DECEMBER JANUARY FEBRUARY   Number 2

A GOOD GAME FOR HOME FUN

In playing *Initials*, those in the game usually sit in a circle. Any number up to forty or fifty may take part. One player gives the initial of the name of some famous person in history. The next player at the right must give a name beginning with the initial and then in turn give the initial of another person in history. If the first player had Columbus in mind, he would say "C" and the second player might name Columbus, Cabot, or Cortez and then, with Washington in mind, he would give the initial "W." Any person failing to do what is called for must sit in the middle of the circle until he can answer when some one else fails.

The game may be played also with the names of birds, animals, vegetables, or flowers, or with those of automobiles.

JOKES

Boy: Father, if you will give me a dime, I will be a good boy.

Father: When I was your age, I was good for nothing.

Small boy: 'Scuse me, aunt! I hate to bother you — but I really think you are sitting on a little snake that I've mislaid. — *Life*.

Bulldog for sale; will eat anything. Very fond of children.

OLD RIDDLES

Full of holes, and full of holes, but still it holds water! *Ans.* A sponge.

On a hill there is a little green house. Inside the little green house is a white house. Inside the white house is a red house. Inside the red house are some little black babies. Can you guess my riddle? *Ans.* A watermelon.

As I was crossing London Bridge, I met a London scholar. He took off his hat and drew off his glove. Please tell me the name of the scholar. *Ans.* Andrew.

The Sphinx's Riddle. What creature walks upon four feet in the morning, upon two at noon, and upon three at night? *Ans.* Man.

A PUZZLE

Find the names of twelve animals:

```
d h r f
c o a x
s t g e
e w l b
```

EDITORIAL TROUBLES

The editors sat in a sad, sad row.
They had no poetry. 'Twas a dreadful blow.
They felt like weeping, but instead they sat
And made this jingle, — now what of that?
    BOARD OF EDITORS

Lost: Saturday morning, May 28, on Lincoln Road between Danville and Pittsfield, a black leather automobile trunk marked R.D.H.   The finder will please notify R. D. Huntington, 12 Riverside Drive, Danville, Illinois.

2. In writing a notice of a meeting, why should a person put in the time and place of the meeting? What should he put in to attract people to the meeting?

3. What should be included in a notice of a lost article?

[Written composition]

4. Write notices of your own similar to those in Exercise 1.   First write a notice connected with a meeting, entertainment, game, or other event connected with your school or with some club to which you belong; then write a notice of a lost or found article.

7. Review and Summary

I. Pronunciation and Meaning of Words

1. First show how each of the words in italics is pronounced and then explain its meaning:

1. Frank made the business letter neat in *appearance*.
2. For a *salutation* he used *Dear Sirs*.
3. For a *complimentary close* he used *Yours truly*.
4. He wrote his *signature* clearly.
5. The address on the *envelope* could be read easily.
6. The *abbreviations* in the address were correct.

2. The word *fine* is often both overworked and misused.   Name substitutes for it that may be used in the following sentences:

1. The weather was fine.
2. The boys had had a fine time.
3. The book was a fine one.
4. The class made a fine record.
5. I am feeling fine, thank you.

II. Writing a Note

3. Copy this note, punctuating it correctly; and then write a note like it to some one who would be glad to hear from you:

271 Summit Avenue Saint Paul Minnesota
January 30 1928

Dear Dick

I have been studying so hard lately that I'm ready for anything   The snowshoeing trip for Saturday strikes me as just right   Let me know when you are to start and I'll be ready

As ever
Philip

III. Preparing a Paper to Keep

4. For the fourth paper to be put with those that you are keeping to be bound together at the end of the year, you may do one of the following things:

a. Make as perfect a copy as possible of the letter you wrote in the lesson beginning on page 183 or in the one beginning on page 185.

b. Copy four or five jokes or conundrums that you would like to keep.

c. Write in the form of a letter a story telling of the winter adventures of a snowbird, of a fox, or of a rabbit. Use as a signature the name of a bird or animal.

8. Mastery of the Sentence.   Test No. 2

Copy the groups of words that form complete sentences:

1. Late in the evening
2. The tree with spreading branches
3. A bird sang gayly
4. When the man stopped his car
5. It was a crowded scene and there were many objects to attract attention
6. A sudden squall struck the sea, ploughing deep white furrows in it, and at the same instant a single piercing shriek
7. Blinded by the lightning, and drenched by the rain, which fell in torrents, we crept to shelter

Find the ends of the sentences; then copy the exercises, putting in the capitals and periods that are needed:

8. No wild animal dies of old age its life has soon or late a tragic end it is only a question of how long it can hold out against its foes.
9. The thieves spoke low but the maidservant heard them she jumped out of bed, and being in the dark, stumbled against the door on hearing the noise the men took to their heels.

Copy the following sentences, inserting in each the marks of punctuation needed to make the thought clear:

10. The Pilgrim Fathers sailed from Plymouth England September 6 1620
11. The soldier carried a sword a flintlock and a powder horn
12. What does this bundle of arrows tied up in a snake skin mean asked the Pilgrims of Squanto

13. It means sirs said he that the Indians wish to make war upon you

Combine the sentences in each exercise below so that they form one clear sentence. You may omit words and add others, but you must not change the thought.

14. In the grove there were oak trees. Poplars were there also and evergreens.

15. The weather was pleasant. The children stayed indoors.

16. The river was swift. It was crossed by a bridge built of stone.

17. The widow was kept busy. She had seven children to care for. She had a farm to manage.

Compare your record with the following score. How can you improve your record if you are not satisfied with it?

Fair, 9–10 correct exercises; *good*, 11–12 correct exercises; *excellent*, 13–17 correct exercises.

9. Three Parts of Speech

I. Words Used in Place of Nouns

1. If we had only nouns to stand for people, our speech would resemble that of a little child who, instead of saying, "I want my ball" says "Baby wants baby's ball" or "Mary wants Mary's ball." We should, for example, be obliged to say in place of "The soldier carried his sword at his side," "The soldier carried the soldier's sword at the soldier's side."

2. Compare the statements in each exercise. Tell

which you like the better and then point out the
words that take the place of nouns.

1. Richard, will Richard take Richard's book home
with Richard?

Richard, will you take your book home with you?

2. Helen began Helen's letter by saying, "Helen has
been on a visit to Helen's aunt."

Helen began her letter by saying, "I have been on
a visit to my aunt."

3. Words like *I*, *my*, *you*, *your*, *he*, *his*, are **pronouns.**

A pronoun is a word used in place of a noun.

4. Tell what person is meant by each pronoun in
italics:

A blind man, having lost *his* way, happened to stum-
ble against a lame man *who* could not get out of the
road.

"Help *me* into the path," said the blind man.

"How can *I* do that," said the lame man, "since *I*
am hardly able to drag *myself* along?   But *you* seem
to be a sturdy fellow.   Suppose *we* join forces.   Take
me on *your* back, and *we* will travel together."

5. Use in sentences, and then name the pronouns:

My brother and I	You and I
He and I	My mother and we children
My sister and I	My uncle and his children
She and I	

6. Notice that the pronouns in the following sentences show possession, or ownership, and that they
are written without an apostrophe:

The fawn had lost *its* mother.

This book is *ours;* that is *theirs.*

This pencil is *hers;* that is *yours.*

7. Write sentences of your own showing how to use the possessive pronouns *its*, *ours*, *theirs*, *hers*, and *yours*.

II. Summary.   Nouns, Pronouns, Verbs

8. Make sure that you understand these definitions and can give other examples for each:

1. A noun is the name of a person, place, or thing. Ex. *boy, Chicago, rock.*

2. A proper noun is the name of a particular person, place, or thing.   Ex. *Theodore Roosevelt, New York, Christmas.*

3. A common noun is a name that may be applied to any one of a class.   Ex. *girl, city, tree.*

4. A noun is singular in number when it means only one.   Ex. *bird, child, river.*

5. A noun is plural in number when it means more than one.   Ex. *knives, toys, houses.*

6. A noun is possessive when it shows ownership. Ex. The *boy's* mittens, the *soldier's* uniform.

7. A singular noun forms its possessive by adding *'s* (apostrophe s).   Ex. *girl's, man's, farmer's.*

> *Exception.* Where it is difficult to pronounce the final syllable with the added *s*, the singular possessive may be formed by the addition of the apostrophe alone.   Ex. *Moses'.*

8. A plural noun ending in *s* forms its possessive by the placing of an apostrophe after the *s*.   Ex. the *boys'* playground, the *soldiers'* camp.

9. A pronoun is a word used in place of a noun. Ex. *he, she, they, you, I, it, who, whom.*

10. A verb is a word used to assert action or being. Ex. (a) *run, jump, think;* (b) *is, seems, looks.*

11. A verb phrase is a group of words used as a verb. Ex. *is playing, have been jumping, can sing, could have gone.*

10. Using Words Correctly — Review for the First Half Year [1]

Test G. Second Form. Twelve Common Errors

Copy statements, filling the blanks with words from the list below No. 4:

1. The scouts ——— their work in the woods.
2. The campers ——— a bear.
3. The bear ——— from a cave among the rocks.
4. When school was dismissed, the children ——— home.

did   seen   came   run
done   saw   come   ran

In completing each answer, use a word that makes sense:

5. Why isn't Mary studying?   She ——— no book.
6. Have you her book? No, I ——— it.

In copying the answers to these questions, complete them with words from the list below Number 12:

7. To whom was the letter sent?   It was sent to my brother and ———.
8. How strong is Helen's brother?   He is stronger than ———.
9. Was it Margaret who came?   No, it wasn't ———.
10. Whom did you and your mother visit?   My mother and ——— visited my grandmother.
11. What do you and your sister like to do in the winter? ——— and ——— like to skate.
12. Where do you and your brother play?   ——— and ——— play in our yard.

me   she   she   me   she   me   him   I
I   her   her   I   her   I   he   me

[1] For alternative tests, see the *Teachers' Manual.*

Test H. Second Form. Giving Words their Right Meaning

Copy and complete these sentences, using words from the list below Number 6:

1. The bridge was ——— a mile long.
2. The distant mountain looked ——— near.
3. Stones were ——— in the path.
4. The pitiful little child looked ———.
5. My sister ——— a book from me.
6. The man ——— his son how to run a farm.

most	very	laying	strange	borrowed	learned
almost	real	lying	funny	lent	taught

Test I. Second Form. Telling What Happened

Copy the second statement in each exercise, using a form of the word in italics to complete it:

1. Toward night the wind *rose*. The wind had ———.
2. A storm *came* from the northeast. A storm had ——— from the northeast.
3. The girls *went* home. The girls had ——— home.
4. The girls *chose* the short way. The girls had ——— the shortest way.
5. The boys *took* the route through the woods. The boys had ——— the route through the woods.
6. The picnickers *sat* under the trees. The picnickers had ——— under the trees.
7. The children *lay* on the grass. The children had ——— on the grass.
8. The class *drew* a map. The class had ——— a map.
9. The children *wrote* invitations. The children had ——— invitations.
10. The boys *saw* a young squirrel. The boys had ——— a young squirrel.

Chapter V — SOME GREAT AMERICANS

1. Abraham Lincoln

[Conversation]

1. The following quotations are a few of the many that might be given to show how men have looked upon the character of Abraham Lincoln:

LINCOLN

Oh, slow to smite and swift to spare,
    Gentle and merciful and just!

WILLIAM CULLEN BRYANT

He built the rail pile as he built the State,
Pouring his splendid strength through every blow.

EDWIN MARKHAM

He had the art of winning with his humor.

RICHARD HENRY STODDARD

He knew no fear except the fear of doing wrong.
ROBERT G. INGERSOLL

The kindly, earnest, brave, foreseeing man,
Sagacious, patient, dreading praise, not blame,
New birth of our new soil, the first American.
JAMES RUSSELL LOWELL

2. Which of the quotations refer to qualities that you admire most? Are there questions about the other quotations that you would like to ask?

3. Can you tell why Lincoln is spoken of as the *first American*?

[Using appropriate words]

4. Notice that the expressions used in the quotations were all carefully chosen. Which do you particularly like?

5. Why, in speaking of Lincoln or any other great man, should a person choose words that are dignified and for that reason sound appropriate? Why should he avoid slang?

6. Choose one of the quotations and explain its meaning; then memorize the quotation.

2. A Lincoln Pantomime

[Learning to study]

1. Many stories similar to the following are told of Lincoln's honesty:

Lincoln at one time kept a country store for a man. As with everything that he undertook for others, Lincoln did his best with the store to make it a success. He was honest, civil, and ready to do anything that would

encourage customers to come to the place. He was
patient, alert, and full of pleasantries.

One afternoon he weighed some tea for a woman.
After she had gone, he looked at the scales and saw
that he had used a wrong weight and had given the
woman too little tea for her money. He weighed out
what was due, and carried it to her.

After closing the store one night, Abraham Lincoln
sat up late counting his money. As he counted, he
found a mistake had been made. He thought a minute; then made up his mind that he must have given a
customer the wrong change. He took from the money
drawer the few cents due the customer, and put the
rest of the money away. He then put on his coat and
hat, and after locking the door behind him, walked a
long distance to return the customer his money.

Lincoln's honesty was strongly illustrated by the
way that he kept his accounts with a law-partner whom
he familiarly addressed as "Billy." One day when his
partner was away, a man came and asked Lincoln to
fill out a paper for him. Lincoln got the paper from
the drawer, filled it out, and gave it to the man, who
paid him for it. Lincoln put half of the fee into his
own pocket, and then carefully wrapped the other half
in a piece of paper, and after labeling it "Billy," he put
it away.

The customer said, "Why do you divide the money
in that way? Why don't you make a record of the
money, and then give your partner his share later?"

Lincoln answered: "Because I promised my mother
never to use money belonging to another person."

2. Think of a good title for each story; then tell
what in the story interested you.

3. Judging from its use, what should you say is the
meaning of each of the words given here in italics?

Lincoln was *civil* to his customers.

He was *patient* and *alert*.

Lincoln's honesty is *illustrated* in the way he kept his accounts with a law-partner whom he *familiarly addressed* as "Billy."

After *labeling* the paper, he put it away.

4. Use the dictionary to help you with the meaning of the words in Exercise 3 about which you have any doubt.

[Stories with pantomime]

5. Plan a program composed of story-telling and pantomime.[1] Have some members of the class tell the stories given in Exercise 1 or other stories like them and then have different boys and girls act the stories without saying a word. The class is to guess each time what story the actor had in mind.

6. In telling a story connected with the pantomime, be careful to select words that are dignified and appropriate.

[Written exercise]

7. Write sentences of your own showing the meaning of the words in Exercise 3 that are printed in italics.

[1] For the pantomine connected with the first story in Exercise 1, a table may be used for the counter, but otherwise none of the things used should be represented. The only character in the pantomime should be that of the child taking the part of Abraham Lincoln. The scene may begin with Abraham Lincoln busying himself about the country store. He may be rolling imaginary barrels into place or arranging imaginary goods on a shelf. The audience is left to imagine the entrance of a woman. Lincoln turns, bows pleasantly, and listens to her order. He goes through the actions of taking a scoop and weighing tea carefully, of wrapping the tea in paper, and of tying string around the parcel. He takes the woman's money, gives her change, bows again, and then turns to his work. After some time he stops suddenly, goes to the scales, sees the wrong weight, gets some tea, weighs it, and puts it into a bag. He then puts on his hat and leaves the store.

3. Making a Booklet about Lincoln

[Conversation]

1. Many Americans are so interested in the character and life of Lincoln that year after year they collect all of the information about him that they can.   You may be interested in helping your class make a similar collection of stories, poems, and pictures of Lincoln and in binding them in a book; or, better still, in making a booklet by yourself.   The principal of your school will be interested in seeing the work when it is done, and another sixth grade will find it of great help.

2. In February the newspapers and magazines are filled with pictures and articles about Lincoln. Where else can you find material for a booklet?

[Written composition]

3. In making a contribution to the class booklet, choose a, b, c, d, or e:

    a. Write in your own words one of the stories given in Lesson 2, page 201.

    b. Write a story that you have heard of Lincoln's kindness, his ambition, or his shrewdness.

    c. Mount a picture connected with Lincoln's life and copy a poem or a number of quotations.

    d. Write a paper telling why you admire Lincoln.

    e. Write a description of Lincoln's birthplace, or write a brief account of his life.

What care will you take in your selection of words?

4. Choose a committee to select, with your teacher's help, the best papers and bind them together.

4. Theodore Roosevelt

[Conversation]

1. Theodore Roosevelt's own character is revealed in his message to American boys.

TO THE BOYS OF AMERICA

Of course what we have a right to expect from the American boy is that he shall turn out to be a good American man. Now, the chances are strong that he won't be much of a man unless he is a good deal of a boy. He must not be a coward or a weakling, a bully, a shirk, or a prig. He must work hard and play hard. He must be clean-minded and clean-lived, and able to hold his own under all circumstances and against all comers. It is only on these conditions that he will grow into the kind of man of whom America can really be proud. In life, as in a football game, the principle to follow is: Hit the line hard; don't foul and don't shirk, but hit the line hard.

ROOSEVELT

2. Roosevelt was not only a political leader but also a great traveler, a scientist, and a writer. Find out from the following stories what helped him to become great.

ROOSEVELT'S STRENGTH

As a boy Theodore Roosevelt was weak. He had asthma so badly that he could not lie down at night. When he was nine years old, he made up his mind to grow strong. He exercised in a gymnasium built on a porch of his home in New York City. Later he lived on a ranch in the west. He rode horseback, he walked, he herded cattle, he hunted. In this way he made his weak body into a strong, robust one that scarcely knew what fatigue meant.

ROOSEVELT'S READING

Roosevelt was a great reader. As a boy, he was fond of books of travel and those telling about birds and wild animals. He was often seen about the house with Stanley's Travels in Africa under one arm and a natural history under the other. As he grew older, he kept his interest in books. Even when he was President and had many responsibilities to carry, he found time to read several hundred books each year. In his travels in Africa he took a library of sixty books. These were bound in pigskin so that they could be carried on donkey back and across the desert without injury.

[Choosing appropriate words]

3. Statements similar to the following are often used in speaking of Roosevelt. Can you give the meaning of the words printed in italics?

Roosevelt was strong and *robust*. He scarcely knew what *fatigue* meant.

Roosevelt was *energetic* and *persistent*. He led a *strenuous* life.

4. Give other words describing Roosevelt's character.

[Giving a talk]

5. Try in one of the following ways to give the class your idea of Roosevelt:

a. Tell in your own words what Roosevelt expected of American boys.

b. Give a talk telling why you admire Roosevelt.

c. With a picture in hand describe a scene such as that of Roosevelt and his Rough Riders, Roosevelt hunting, or Roosevelt traveling with John Burroughs; then show the class the picture.

d. Find in a book of reference a story to tell of Roosevelt's travels, of his interest in birds, of his letters to his children, or some other story. Make a report to the class.

e. Tell how Lincoln and Roosevelt differed in character and what American boys and girls can learn from each.

In preparing your talk, be careful to choose words that fit your meaning and sound appropriate.

[Written work]

6. Sum up in one or two sentences each of the paragraphs in Exercises 1 and 2.

5. Review and Summary

I. Pronunciation and Meaning of Words

1. Give the correct pronunciation of the following words; then show the meaning of each by using the word in a sentence describing some character in history:

merciful	energetic	just	civil
courageous	spirited	truthful	kindly

II. Proof-Reading. Proper Names

2. Find the proper names:

THREE GREAT AMERICAN WOMEN

Anne Hutchinson joined the Massachusetts Bay Colony in 1634. She was the first leader among women in America.

Julia Ward Howe wrote the *Battle Hymn of the Republic*.

Clara Barton founded the American Red Cross Society sixteen years after the close of the Civil War.

3. Study the sentences in Exercise 2 until you can write them correctly with your book closed.

III. Writing a Paper to Keep

4. In deciding upon a subject for a paper to be prepared and then bound with others at the end of the year, you may write some talk that you have given recently, or you may write your favorite story of Benjamin Franklin, Abraham Lincoln, Theodore Roosevelt, or of a great American woman.

5. Write the paper neatly and then proof-read it to make sure that you have placed a period at the end of each sentence and written each proper name correctly.   What care will you take in your choice of words?

6. The Verb and its Subject

I

1. As you learned on page 181, the verb is a word asserting action or being of some particular thing. Notice that in the following sentence the assertion is made about soldiers:

The soldiers camped near the river.

The noun *soldiers* is the subject of the verb *camped*.

2. Name the verbs and their subjects:

1. The canoe floated down the stream.
2. Clouds hid the sun.
3. A dog barked.
4. The boys ran home.
5. Birds were singing.
6. A whistle blew.
7. The children ran away.
8. A car turned the corner.

3. Sometimes, as in the following sentences, the subject of a verb is made up of a group of words:

> The flag above the schoolhouse waved in the breeze.
> A procession of soldiers passed the house.

If you were to find the one word in each group that really names the subject, you would choose *flag* as the subject of the verb *waved*, and *procession* as the subject of the verb *passed*. *The flag waved. The procession passed.*

4. Find in each of the following sentences the verb and then the one word used as its simple subject. Read the sentence; then name the word subject and the verb. Read: *The eagle in the sky flew in circles.* Say: *Eagle flew.*

1. The stars in the milky way shone bright.
2. The snow on the ground sparkled.
3. On the frozen river children skated.
4. The wind from the north blew hard.
5. Near the river a bonfire burned brightly.
6. The boys on the ice played hockey.
7. The children at home read books.
8. The men on the streets hurried home.
9. The clock in the church tower struck nine.
10. During the night, snow fell.
11. After the storm the ship sailed away.
12. In the deep forest lived many shy wood birds.
13. Rabbits hid among the bushes.
14. An owl hooted at night from the branches of a pine tree.
15. The hunter's dog guarded his cabin.

[Written work]

5. Write for each sentence in Exercise 4 its word subject and its verb.

II

[Using the right verb]

6. Notice that in the following sentences *is*, *was*, and *has* are each used with a subject that means one person or thing, and that *are*, *were*, and *have* are used with a subject that means more than one:

The cloud *is* dark.   The clouds *are* dark.
The road *was* muddy.   The roads *were* muddy.
The soldier *has* a knapsack.   The soldiers *have* knapsacks.

Is, *was*, and *has* are singular in number and are used with subjects that are singular.
Are, *were*, and *have* are plural verbs and are used with subjects that are plural.

A verb must agree with its subject in number.

7. Complete:

1. The man is at work.   The men ——— at work.
2. The street is empty.   The streets ——— empty.
3. A star is shining.   Stars ——— shining.
4. The child has gone home.   The children ——— gone home.
5. The cloud has disappeared.   The clouds ——— disappeared.
6. The cabin was built of logs.   Cabins ——— built of logs.
7. The Puritan was strict.   Puritans ——— strict.
8. The pioneer was courageous.   Pioneers ——— courageous.
9. Was the boy late?   ——— the boys late?

8. Give pairs of sentences of your own showing the use of *is* and *are*, *was* and *were*, and *has* and *have*.

9. Decide which subjects require a singular verb and which require a plural verb and then complete each sentence:

1. A brass key ———— fastened to Franklin's kite.
2. Printing presses in olden days ———— crude.
3. One of Franklin's brothers ———— a printer.
4. Another brother ———— a sailor.
5. A basket of supplies ———— carried to the soldiers.
6. Only one of the nurses ———— able to help the wounded soldiers.

7. Using Words Correctly

Test J. First Form. Speaking of One or More

Copy and complete, using words from the list below Number 5:

1. A flock of birds ———— flying overhead.
2. The oxen ———— hauling heavy logs.
3. One of the boys ———— lost in the woods.
4. The crows in the tree ———— cawing.
5. Neither one of the girls ———— come.

is	is	was	was	have
are	are	were	were	has

Use words from below Number 10 in completing these sentences:

6. Each of the miners ———— a lantern.
7. Every boy in the class ———— ready.
8. ———— there any books left?
9. ———— all of the boys there?
10. ———— either of the girls returned?

have	was	isn't	wasn't	**haven't**
has	were	aren't	weren't	**hasn't**

For Practice Exercises see pages 285 and 286.

Chapter VI — A TRAVEL CLUB

1. Planning a Travel Club

Our country contains many natural wonders of which every American can be proud. To learn something new of its glaciers, high waterfalls, giant trees, and deep canyons, your class will enjoy forming a travel club and taking imaginary trips to different places.

Beside the material given in this chapter and in your geographies, you will have use for illustrated magazines and books of travel, and also for guidebooks and booklets issued by different railroad companies (see page 188).

After collecting your material, decide how you can use it to the best advantage.

2. A Dangerous Climb

I

[Learning to study]

1. Glaciers are great fields of ice formed by the melting and freezing of the snow of many winters. These fields, which are often found in mountain valleys, move forward each year, carrying boulders, trees, and débris with them. The motion, however, is so slow that it cannot be seen, but from beneath the glacier can be heard the cracking and grinding of ice, mingled with the sound of flowing water.

2. In crossing a glacier, travelers have to be on their guard against deep cracks, or crevasses. These

crevasses are often hundreds of feet deep, and since new ones are continually forming, travelers find them at unexpected places. Judging from the picture, how do you think men go prepared for the dangers they may encounter in crossing a glacier? Why are the men warmly clad? Why do they wear shoes with spikes in them? Why do they carry rope and staffs?

3. With the help of Exercises 1 and 2 be ready to give in turn with your classmates the information called for in this outline:

Glaciers

I. What glaciers are; where found; movement.

II. The dangers encountered in crossing a glacier; from the cold; from known crevasses; from new and unknown crevasses.

III. How men go prepared to cross a glacier; ————,
————.

4. Some of the most famous glaciers are in Glacier National Park in Wyoming.   Others, such as the Muir Glacier and the Malespina, are in Alaska.   What books can you consult for information about these?

5. What impressions do you get of an Alaskan glacier from the following selection?

CROSSING AN ALASKAN GLACIER

About three miles above the front of the glacier I climbed to the surface of it by means of axe-steps.   As far as the eye could reach, the level, or nearly level, glacier stretched away indefinitely beneath the gray sky, a seemingly boundless prairie of ice.   No trace of the west shore was visible, and in case the clouds should settle and give snow, or the wind again become violent, I feared getting caught in a tangle of crevasses. Watching the weather, I sauntered about on the crystal sea.   For a mile or two I found the ice remarkably safe.

Thus encouraged, I at last pushed out for the other side.   Toward the west side I came to a closely crevassed section in which I had to make long, narrow tacks and doublings, tracing the edges of tremendous crevasses, many of them from twenty to thirty feet wide and perhaps a thousand feet deep — beautiful and awful.

JOHN MUIR

6. What expressions in the story help you most in gaining an idea of the glacier?

7. Judging from its use, what should you say was the meaning of each of the following words?

The glacier seemed a *boundless* prairie of ice.
I feared getting caught in a *tangle* of crevasses.
I *sauntered* about on the *crystal* sea.
I made long narrow *tacks* and *doublings*.

8. If you are uncertain of the meaning that you have given to the words in Exercise 7, you should look them up in a dictionary.

[Giving a talk]

9. Use one of these suggestions to help you in planning a talk or "lecture" on glaciers:

a. Make the story in Exercise 5 clear to your class by telling it in your own words.

b. With the help of the outline in Exercise 2 give a lecture on glaciers. Use pictures to illustrate your talk.

c. Give a lecture on some glacier about which you have read.

d. Tell of an imaginary adventure in climbing a mountain and crossing a glacier.

10. Appoint critics to make reports at the end of the meeting. Have one critic tell which speakers gave the most valuable information; have another one tell which speakers planned their talks most carefully; and have a third critic tell in what ways some of the lectures could be improved.

II

[Writing in paragraphs]

11. Tell why the story in Exercise 5 is written in two paragraphs.

12. In the outline in Exercise 3 how many main topics are covered? In how many paragraphs should a paper that follows the outline be written?

13. Write the paragraphs called for by the outline in Exercise 3, page 213.

3. High Waterfalls and Deep Canyons

[Learning to study]

1. Travelers come from all over the world to view our two great natural wonders, Niagara Falls and the Colorado Canyon. Where do they go to see these wonders? For what is each place famous?

2. What idea of Niagara do you gain from this description?

THE FALLS OF NIAGARA

The Falls of Niagara, among the greatest in the world, occur in the Niagara River as it flows from Lake Erie into Lake Ontario. Other waterfalls are higher but none contains such a volume of water. Over the cliffs the water from four of the Great Lakes flows ceaselessly with a thunderous roar that can be heard for miles. So powerful is the downpour that the water breaks into foam and at the foot of the falls throws up a great cloud of mist, through which, on sunshiny days, rainbows continually shine.

The falls are divided by Goat Island into the American Falls and the Canadian, or Horseshoe Falls. The most beautiful section of the American Falls is the Bridal Veil, so called because it resembles a gigantic wedding veil. The famous Horseshoe Falls are noted for their wonderful color. When played upon by the sunshine, they show the deep green of the ocean, the blue of the sky, and iridescent colors that match the rainbows in the mist below.

Visitors are able to see the falls from above, from below, and even from behind. They drive through the Park and get fine views of both the Bridal Veil and the Horseshoe Falls; they take a small boat called the Maid of the Mist and see the falls from the river, and they put on raincoats and enter the slippery path that takes them into the Cave of Winds behind a section of the waterfall.

3. Tell what you think would impress you most about the falls of Niagara, and then, with the help of others in your class, be ready to give in turn the facts called for in this outline:

Niagara Falls

I. The falls: rank, location, source of water, signs of power.

II. The two famous sections and their characteristics: ———, ———.

III. The three views visitors get of the falls: ———, ———, ———.

4. With the help of this paragraph find what makes the Colorado Canyon impressive:

THE COLORADO CANYON

The Colorado Canyon, which is situated in the south-western part of the United States, is one of the most impressive canyons in the world. It is over two hundred fifty miles in length, thirteen miles across, and from three thousand to six thousand feet in depth. The trail down is seven miles long, and the trip down and back a full day's journey. When you first look into the canyon, you see nothing but colored rocks and a blue mist; but, when you look more carefully, you see in the depths, thousands of feet below, the turbulent stream that has been at work for thousands of years cutting its way through solid rock.

5. If you wished to give a person a clear idea of the Colorado Canyon, why should you tell its location? What else should you say?

[Giving a talk]

6. For your travel talk on waterfalls and canyons choose a, b, c, or d:

a. With the help of the outline in Exercise 3, prepare a talk on Niagara Falls.

b. Tell the story of a visit to Niagara Falls by some one whom you know, or tell of an imaginary trip there.

c. Compare the Falls of the Yosemite with those of the Yellowstone.

d. Give a description of the Colorado Canyon or that of the Yellowstone, or make a comparison of the two.

[Writing in paragraphs]

7. Write as much of the description of Niagara Falls as you can remember. How many main topics are there in the outline in Exercise 3? In how many paragraphs should the description be written?

4. Travel Letters

[Making plans]

1. Choose one of the famous places mentioned in the following list, or some other place, and write a travel letter telling of a real or an imaginary visit there:

Places of remarkable scenery: Yellowstone Park, the Yosemite Valley, the Garden of the Gods, Royal Gorge, Glacier Park, the Valley of Ten Thousand Smokes, Muir Woods, Grant Park, Sequoia National Park, Mariposa Grove.

Places showing remarkable formations: Petrified Forest (Arizona), Natural Bridge (the one in Virginia and the one in Utah), Crater Lake, Mesa Verde, Devil's Tower, Devil's Profile, Mammoth Cave, the Old Man of the Mountain.

Places of historical interest: the Old Mission, Santa Barbara, California; Santa Fe, Texas; St. Augustine, Florida; Starved Rock, Illinois; Mackinac Island, Michigan; Jamestown, Virginia; Plymouth, Massachusetts; Lexington and Concord, Massachusetts; Mount Vernon, Virginia; Lincoln's birthplace, Hodgkinsville, Kentucky.

2. To get an idea of what to say in describing an imaginary trip, look at pictures and read descriptions such as you will find in travel circulars, geographical magazines, geographies, and encyclopedias.

[Writing a letter]

3. Write your letter to the class. Try to make the boys and girls see what you are describing. Choose only one or two things to tell about and give enough details to make the description clear. What will determine the number of paragraphs in your letter?

5. Review and Summary

I. Pronunciation and Meaning of Words

1. Notice the division of each of the following words by syllable; then pronounce the word:

glacier (gla cier)	Niagara (Ni ag a ra)
traveler (trav el er)	thunderous (thun der ous)
crevasse (cre vasse)	ceaselessly (cease less ly)
boundless (bound less)	canyon (can yon)
volume (vol ume)	situated (sit u a ted)

2. Show the meaning of words in Exercise 1 by using them in sentences describing some of the natural wonders of our country.

II. Proof-Reading — Paragraphing

3. Write an outline giving the three main topics covered by this description:

The Western States are made up almost entirely of mountains and plateaus.

Most of the surface is more than a mile above sea level and many of the peaks are two or three miles in height.

The eastern portion is a continuation of the great plains which reach to the very base of the Rocky Mountains.

These mountains extend across the country into Mexico in the south and Canada in the north.

They are made up of a large number of ranges and ridges which attain their greatest height in Colorado.

In the western portion are other systems of mountains.

Running parallel with the Rockies is the system of mountains called the Sierra Nevada in California and the Cascade Ranges in Oregon.

Beyond these lie the Coast Ranges which in places rise directly out of the ocean.

4. Write the paragraph that goes with the three sections of your outline.

III. Writing a Paper to Keep

5. In preparing the paper to be bound with others at the end of the year, you may copy your travel letter or write one of the talks that you prepared for your travel 'club. Try to find a picture to illustrate your paper and to mount it neatly. Make sure that your paper is written in paragraphs and without errors.

6. Picture-Making Words

I. The Adjective

1. To impress a person with the size of a canyon, you might call it gigantic, huge, or immense.

2. What words might you use to describe a trail into a canyon if you wished to bring out the fact that it is dangerous?

3. Notice how the words in italics in the following sentence help to give a picture of the ice in a glacier:

The ice in the glacier was *blue*, *clear* as crystal, and *hard*.

4. Picture-making words like *blue*, *clear*, and *hard* are called **adjectives.**

5. Tell what is described in each of the following sentences by the adjectives in italics:

A *bright* rainbow shone in the mist.

In the park grew *tall* trees.

A *roaring* cataract raced down the mountain side.

6. Each adjective in Exercise 6 describes some object, that is, it is used with a noun. The adjective *bright*, for example, is used with the noun *rainbow*. *Bright* limits, or modifies, the meaning of *rainbow* by showing that only one kind is meant, a *bright* one.

An adjective is a word used to modify the meaning of a noun or pronoun.

7. Make a list of adjectives describing each object and person named:

1. Flowers. Begin with *fragrant*.
2. Birds. Begin with *young*.
3. Weather. Begin with *stormy*.
4. Boys. Begin with *strong*.
5. Girls. Begin with *capable*.

8. Try to make the meaning of each sentence clearer by filling the blank with an adjective:

1. Over the ——— cliff fell a stream of water.
2. ——— colors shone in the mist.
3. ——— trees grew near the stream.
4. The ——— roar of the falls could be heard for miles.
5. A ——— bridge crossed the stream.

9. The following game calls for many adjectives. Use it to help you in becoming familiar with them:

GAME: *The Minister's Cat*

In playing *The Minister's Cat*, each person when his turn comes, gives an adjective describing a cat. All possible adjectives beginning with *a* are used, then those beginning with *b*, and next those beginning with *c*, and so on through the alphabet. The first player may say: "The minister's cat was an *angry* cat." The next may say: "The minister's cat was an *aged* cat (or *alley* cat, or *amiable* cat)." If a player cannot think of another adjective beginning with the letter that is being used, he gives a word beginning with the next letter in the alphabet.

10. Franklin was thrifty, industrious, wise, and patriotic. Give adjectives that name the opposite qualities to those that helped him in winning success. Ex. thrifty, wasteful.

11. Play the game described on page 224; then write an opposite for each adjective named here:

	List I		*List II*
1.	A generous man	21.	A fierce animal
2.	A strong horse	22.	Cold water
3.	An unselfish woman	23.	A sunshiny day
4.	A young bird	24.	A heavy package
5.	A swift runner	25.	A thoughtful person
6.	A good baby	26.	A kind aunt
7.	A careful worker	27.	A cheerful person
8.	A thrifty girl	28.	A beautiful flower
9.	A new machine	29.	A cross woman
10.	A healthy plant	30.	An intelligent man
11.	A patient worker	31.	A persistent inventor
12.	A studious boy	32.	An enterprising worker
13.	A proud woman	33.	A patriotic soldier
14.	A wicked person	34.	A lazy boy
15.	A timorous person	35.	A loyal friend
16.	A capable worker	36.	An ancient city
17.	A shrinking income	37.	An alert waitress
18.	A strenuous person	38.	A civil conductor
19.	A mighty force	39.	A wise leader
20.	A courteous child	40.	A difficult situation

GAME: *Opposites*

To play the game of *Opposites*, the members in one half of the class sit with books closed while the players in the other half take turns reading aloud the adjectives in List No. I and calling for an opposite of each adjective read.   The score of correct answers is counted; then the players belonging to the half that has been sitting with closed books, open their books and read the adjectives in List No. II, calling in turn on the other half of the class for the opposites of the words given.

II. Articles

12. *A*, *an*, and *the* are adjectives which are used so often that they are given a special name.   They are called **articles.**

13. Point out the articles in these sentences, naming the noun with which each is used:

> The man stood near an oak.
> In his hand he carried a bundle.

The article *an* is used before words beginning with the vowels *a*, *e*, *i*, *o*, *u*.   The article *a* is used before words beginning with consonants, such as, *b*, *c*, *d*, and *f*.

III. Using Adjectives Correctly

14. In comparing objects, we change the form of an adjective.   We may say the sky was *blue* in the morning, *bluer* in the afternoon, and *bluest* in the evening; or, we may say the violet is a *fragrant* flower, the rose is *more fragrant*, and that of all the common garden flowers the lily is the *most fragrant*.

15. In expressing a comparison with adjectives of

one syllable, we often use words ending in *er* or *est*.
We say:

soft	good	rich	sweet
softer	better	richer	sweeter
softest	best	richest	sweetest

16. In expressing a comparison with adjectives of
two or more syllables, we often use the words *more*
or *most*.   We say:

beautiful	intelligent
more beautiful	more intelligent
most beautiful	most intelligent

17. How many persons are compared in the first
sentence?   In the second sentence?

> Fred is taller than his brother.
> Of the three boys in the family John is the brightest.

In comparing two persons or things, we use words
ending in *er*.   In comparing three or more persons
or things, we use words ending in *est*.

18. Complete each sentence using one of the words
given below Number 6:

1. Of the two girls Helen is the ———.
2. Of all the boys in the team Fred is the ———.
3. Of the two brothers, John is the ———.
4. Of the two kinds of candy, the chocolate is the
———.
5. Of the two animals, a tiger is the ———.
6. Of the three soldiers, the Colonel was the ———.

quicker	slower	stronger	better	fiercer	braver
quickest	slowest	strongest	best	fiercest	bravest

19. When is the word *more* used in expressing a
comparison?   When is the word *most* used?

20. Complete, using *more* or *most:*

    7. Of all animals the elephant is the ——— intelligent.

    8. John has a pony and a dog.   The pony is the ——— troublesome.

    9. Mary has a dog and a cat.   The dog is the ——— faithful.

21. Compare:

    10. A horse and a mule as to stubbornness.
    11. A hare and a tortoise as to fleetness.
    12. A cat and a kitten as to playfulness.
    13. A tiger and other animals as to ferocity.
    14. A deer and other animals as to timidity.

7. Using Words Correctly

Test K.   First Form.   Avoiding Senseless Expressions

Copy and complete, using words from the list below Number 4.

    1. The boy went to the circus ———.
    2. Tom's desk is ——— Dick's desk.
    3. The flower was ——— daisy.
    4. I should ——— better.

on a pass	behind	a kind of a	of known
on a free pass	in back of	a kind of	have know

Complete these statements with words from below Number 8.

    5. The boys ——— planned better.
    6. We ——— to take risks.
    7. The boys ran ——— they were frightened.
    8. My brother ——— yet.

could have	ought not	like	did not go
could a	hadn't ought	as if	has not gone

Chapter VII — NATURE–LOVERS

1. A Great Nature-Lover

[Conversation]

1. Among American naturalists there seems to be some luck in the name of John, for three out of the five most famous men have it — John Audubon, John Burroughs, and John Muir. The other two men in the list are Louis Agassiz and Henry Thoreau.

All of these naturalists have been interested in the study of the plants and animal life of our country, but to John Muir belongs special credit for his explorations in Alaska and elsewhere, and for his efforts to preserve the Big Trees and other scenic wonders of California.

[Learning to study]

2. The following biography gives the leading facts in John Muir's life:

JOHN MUIR

John Muir was born in Scotland in 1838, but at the age of eleven he was brought to America when his parents emigrated to make a home in the back woods of Wisconsin. As a boy he delighted in birds and other wild creatures, but there was so much farm work to be done that he had little time for roaming. He was set at ploughing when only twelve years old. Later, like Abraham Lincoln, he split rails for fences. As he grew older, he was able to split a hundred oak rails a day.

When he was about fifteen, Muir began to hunger for knowledge. He borrowed books from the neighbors and saved money and bought some for himself. He read till bedtime, which came all too soon after supper, and as much longer as he could. His father, who was a kind but strict man, forbade his sitting up late. He said, "If you will read, get up as early as you like." After that, early rising was the order of the boy's day, much to the dismay of his father. To make sure of getting up early, John invented a wooden clock to tip him out of bed when the time for rising came.

When he was twenty-two, Muir went to Madison to work his way through Wisconsin University. When he left the university, he said, "I am only leaving one university for another, the Wisconsin University for the University of the Wilderness."

It was not immediately after graduating, however, that he could follow his desire to enter the University of the Wilderness and travel as a naturalist. To get money he had at first to work in a factory.

Finally he started on a botanizing trip in Illinois and Wisconsin. Later, after long walking trips through Indiana, Kentucky, Tennessee, Georgia, and Florida, he went across Panama by rail and from there to San Francisco by ship. From San Francisco he went on foot to the Yosemite, there to find the chief work of his life.

In the Yosemite, Muir spent five whole years and

five more summers, earning his living by superintending a flock of sheep and later by running a sawmill.   His wants were few.   On a little bread and a little tea he would make long journeys on foot over the Sierra, sleeping out without a tent.

At first in the Yosemite Muir devoted himself to botany, but soon he became interested in the great problem of the formation of the beautiful valley.   One day he found a glacier among the mountains and realized that the problem was solved.   The valley had been made by glacial action.   From this time on his interest turned to the subject of glaciers.   He made several trips to Alaska to study the glaciers there.

Muir wrote a number of books.   The titles give an idea of his interests as a naturalist.   They are: *The Mountains of California, Our National Parks, Stickeen, My First Summer in the Sierra, The Yosemite, The Story of My Boyhood and Youth, Travels in Alaska.* Muir died in 1914.

3. What impresses you most about the life of John Muir?   In what way did his boyhood resemble Lincoln's?   How did it prepare him for later life?

[Outlining talks]

4. If you were to make a list of paragraph topics that would help you in telling the story of Muir's life what should you include?

5. The story of Audubon's life is interesting and so is that of Agassiz, of Burroughs, and of Thoreau. Perhaps different groups of three or four members of the class will each volunteer to look up the life of one of these naturalists.

6. In planning a report on Audubon, one person could tell when and where he was born and where he spent most of his life; another could tell of his trips

to the wilderness to study birds of which nothing was known; and a third person could tell about his famous bird pictures and their publication. How could you divide the life of Agassiz? Of Burroughs? Of Thoreau?

[Giving a talk]

7. In making a report to your class, follow a plan of your own or one of these:

a. With the help of others in your class tell the story of John Muir by relays, each giving a paragraph.

b. Tell how the boyhood of John Muir resembled that of Lincoln and how in each case the boyhood helped to prepare the man for the work that he did later.

c. Find a picture of the Yosemite Valley in your geography or elsewhere. Give a description of the valley and tell of John Muir's life there.

d. Tell the story of some other naturalist's life either by yourself or with the help of other members of your class.

[Written work]

8. Select what you consider the most interesting paragraph in the story of John Muir's life on page 228. Study it and then write it from memory.

2. Pictures in Verse

I

[Conversation]

1. Poets, as well as naturalists, help us to enjoy nature. They open our eyes to the beauty in common things, and they lead us to think wise thoughts and to feel fine sentiments.

2. If you have ever been glad to have winter leave

and spring arrive, you will understand the feeling expressed in this poem:

WILD GEESE

The wind blows, the sun shines, the birds sing loud,
The blue, blue sky is flecked with fleecy dappled cloud,
Over earth's rejoicing fields the children dance and sing,
And the frogs pipe in chorus, "It is spring!   It is
    spring!"

The grass comes, the flower laughs where lately lay the
    snow,
O'er the breezy hill-top hoarsely calls the crow,
By the flowing river the alder catkins swing,
And the sweet song-sparrow cries, "Spring!   It is
    spring!"

Hark, what a clamor goes winging through the sky!
Look, children!   Listen to the sound so wild and high!
Like a peal of broken bells, — kling, klang, kling, —
Far and high the wild geese cry, "Spring!   It is
    spring!"

CELIA THAXTER

3. What other name than *Wild Geese* might be given this poem?   Why is *Wild Geese* appropriate?

4. What signs of spring are named in the first stanza?   In each of the others?

[Pictures with words]

5. In the first stanza the repetition of the adjective *blue* makes you feel how *blue* the sky seemed; the words *flecked*, *fleecy*, and *dappled* show that there were only a few light, thin clouds dotting the sky.   What words throughout the poem give you an idea of motion?   Which give you an idea of sound?

6. The haunts of the birds described here are all different in character.   Name the scene pictured in each stanza.

THE SEA-BIRD

Bird of nervous wing and bright
  Flashing silvery to the sun,
Sporting with the sea-foam white,
  When will thy wild course be done?

THE KINGFISHER

His palace is the brake
Where rushes shine and shake.
His music is the murmur of the stream
And the leaf-rustle where the lilies dream.

MAURICE THOMPSON

THE HAWK

And up through the rifted tree-tops
  That signalled the wayward breeze
I saw the hulk of the hawk becalmed
  Far out on the azure seas.

JAMES WHITCOMB RILEY

TO A CITY PIGEON

Why dost thou sit on the heated eaves
And forsake the wood with its freshen'd leaves?
Why dost thou haunt the sultry street
When the paths of the forest are cool and sweet?

WILLIS

7. Give in a few sentences a clear picture (1) of a scene suggested in *Wild Geese* or in one of the stanzas in Exercise 6; or (2) of the haunts of a humming bird, a brown thrush, or some other bird.

II

8. In writing verse, poets frequently use rhyme, but not always. In the first stanza of *Wild Geese*, *cloud* rhymes with *loud* and *spring* with *ring*. Find in the other stanzas the words at the end of the lines that rhyme.

9. Which words rhyme in the stanzas in Exercise 6?

10. Think of words to rhyme with each pair given here:

blowing	spring	west
growing	bring	breast

11. Complete:

> Above the clouds I lift my wing,
> And as I soar I gayly ———.

> The cock is crowing,
> The stream is ———.

> The small birds twitter,
> The lake doth ———.

> All through the winter's storms and cold,
>   Some furry babies swung
> In cradle beds of shining brown
>   On willow branches ———.

12. With the help of the class write a stanza imitating one of those in Exercises 6 or 11. Choose as a subject a flower, a bird, or a spring morning and decide first of all what you would like to say. Select words that will help others to picture the scene and then try to make the stanza sound musical. Do

not feel troubled if you cannot make the lines rhyme.
Ideas and melody are more important.

3. Review and Summary

I. Pronunciation and Meaning of Words

1. First show that you can pronounce each word;
then, in order to show the meaning of the words, use
them in sentences:

Audubon (Au du bon)   exploration (ex plo ra tion)
wilderness (wil der ness)   university (u ni ver si ty)
prairie (prai rie)   botany (bot an y)
naturalist (nat ur al ist)   biography (bi og ra phy)

II. Proof-Reading.   Writing Verse

2. First study the third stanza of the poem called
Wild Geese on page 231, paying particular attention to the punctuation.   Then with your book
closed write the stanza as it is dictated to you.

III. Writing a Paper to Keep

3. In deciding what paper you will prepare so that
it can be bound with others at the end of the year,
keep in mind (1) the verse that you have been writing, (2) the biography that you gave in the lesson
beginning on page 227.

4. School News.   Spring Number

After electing editors for the *Spring Number* of the
School News, try to submit to them a news item, a
nature observation, a springtime story, or a poem.

SCHOOL NEWS — SPRING•NUMBER

VOLUME I   MARCH APRIL MAY   NUMBER 3

EDITORIAL

Now is the time to watch for birds and to observe other life in the fields and woods. In your study you will find these books helpful:

What Bird is That? Chapman

Bird Neighbors. Neltje Blanchan

Everyday Birds. Bradford Torrey

Moths and Butterflies. Dickerson

How to Know the Wild Flowers. Frances T. Parsons

AFTER THE SNOW

On Sunday, the last of March, there was such a thick blanket of snow over the ground that I threw out crumbs for the birds. You should have seen the birds that came to get them!

The first ones to come were some of the prettiest little fox sparrows that I ever saw. This is the time of year when they migrate northward. You can tell them by their reddish brown feathers, the color of a fox, mixed with the gray ones on their backs.

The next to come were some slate-colored juncos. They were very fat jolly chaps with slate-colored beaks, heads, and backs, but with white underneath. Their bright yellow eyes show up very plainly against their dark heads. Their outer tail feathers, which are white, are very noticeable when the birds fly.

Besides these came some song-sparrows, chipping sparrows, grackles and a big fat robin. The birds must have been hungry, for it was not long before they had eaten all of the crumbs and I had to throw them some more.

BUTTERFLY SONG

On the twig of a maple tree
    Lay a caterpillar brown.
He felt the nights were growing cold,
    And the leaves were falling down.

So he spun a silken cradle
    And in it he went to sleep;
And there he stayed all winter long,
    While the snow lay soft and deep.

But when the sun grew warm,
    And the birds began to sing,
He pushed aside the silken thread,
    And spread his painted wing.

PETS' DAY COMING

Pets' Day is coming, boys and girls! Get ready for it. Don't let your pets stray away before the day comes. Bring all the pets you can manage. We will have a big parade just as we had last year. Bring Polly, the parrot; Jack, the dog; Whitie, the cat; Betty, the rabbit; Penny Lenny, the hen; also her chicks, Dot, Red, Blackie and Barney. Don't forget the day, Saturday, May 12, for we are all to have a good time.

5. Words Describing Actions

I. The Adverb

1. An act, such as writing, may be done in many different ways. A boy may write poorly, well, hastily, slowly, painstakingly, carelessly, legibly, or illegibly.

2. Name ways in which a boy can speak. Begin with *politely.*

3. Tell of ways:

In which a girl can sing. Begin with *softly.*
In which a boy can run. Begin with *hurriedly.*
In which a dog can eat. Begin with *greedily.*
In which a man can work. Begin with *steadily.*
In which a child can play. Begin with *hard.*

4. Tell what action is described by each word in italics:

The fire burned *brightly.*
The men started *late.*
The children ran *away.*

5. The words *brightly*, *late*, and *away* are used in the sentences in Exercise 4 with verbs. They are called **adverbs.**

The word adverb (ad-verb) means joined to a verb. An adverb gets its name from the fact that it is most often used with a verb. It may be used also with an adjective or with another adverb.

Examples:

An adverb used with an adjective: The rose was *very* fragrant.

An adverb used with an adverb: The boy started *too* late.

An adverb is a word used to modify the meaning of a verb, an adjective, or another adverb.

6. Can you add to the interest of this story by filling blanks with adverbs answering the questions *How? When? Where?* and *How much?*

"I feel ———," muttered Reddy Fox, "that Peter Rabbit will not be able to stay at home ———. He'll leave his briar patch and come up ——— for some cabbage leaves, and when he crawls through the fence, he will receive a ——— great surprise."

The sun dropped behind the hills and the dark shadows crept ——— across the meadow. The fox, with one eye on the opening in the fence, waited ——— for the little rabbit to appear. ——— he saw what looked like a small shadow, but it wasn't creeping; it was bobbing along ——— fast. Every minute or two it stopped; then it bobbed along ———.

"——— comes my dinner," thought the fox. "I wish Peter Rabbit would hurry ———. He can't get here ——— soon to please me."[1]

7. Write another paragraph to the story. Tell how the rabbit escaped the danger that awaited him. Use these adverbs somewhere in your part of the story: *timidly, very much, quickly, safely.*

II. Game of Opposite Adverbs

8. Notice that the two adverbs printed in italics here express opposite ideas:

The men worked *rapidly*. The men worked *slowly*.

9. Take turns with your classmates in giving the following sentences. Read a sentence and call upon some one to give the sentence, using an adverb which

[1] Adapted from *Bedtime Stories*, copyrighted 1920 by Thornton Burgess.

expresses the opposite idea from the one the sentence already contains. Example: The man spoke courteously. The man spoke rudely.

1. The horse waited patiently.
2. The man spoke angrily.
3. The girl did her work carefully.
4. The boy lifted the baby gently.
5. The boy spoke politely.
6. The child walked gracefully.
7. The musician played well.
8. The mouse crept boldly along the wall.
9. The cub ate hastily.
10. The dog barked fiercely.
11. The children walked swiftly.
12. The children played quietly.
13. The boy spoke cheerfully.
14. The boy answered firmly.
15. The girl whispered softly.
16. The man worked industriously.
17. The man acted harshly.
18. John did the work thoroughly.
19. Fred spoke distinctly.
20. The girl answered rudely.

10. Write sentences containing adverbs opposite in meaning to those given above..

III. Telling an Adverb from an Adjective

1. Adjectives and adverbs are sometimes confused. In order to use the correct word, remember that adverbs frequently end in *ly*. It is correct to say:

The carpenter was *skillful*. He worked *skillfully*.

Skillful is an adjective modifying the noun *carpenter*.

Skillfully is an adverb modifying the verb *worked*.

2. Complete, using an adverb:

    1. The river was swift.   It flowed ———.
    2. The traveler was weary.   He walked ———.
    3. The dog was fierce.   He fought ———.
    4. The rabbit was timid.   It ran ———.
    5. The girls were courteous.   They spoke ———.
    6. The boys were steady **workers**.   They worked ———.
    7. The man was impatient.   He spoke ———.
    8. The woman was angry.   She spoke ———.
    9. The children were merry.   They laughed ———.
    10. Grandmother was generous.   She gave ———.

3. The word *good* is usually an adjective.   It is never an adverb.   The word *well* may be used as an adverb.   It is correct to say:

The children were *good* readers.   They read *well*.

4. Give at least five pairs of sentences of your own showing how *good* and *well* may be used.

Optional Work: The Phrase

Instead of describing our actions by the use of one word, we may use a group of words.   We may say:

The boy ran *into the house.*
The cattle fed *in a pasture.*
The house was built *of brick.*

1. Such expressions as *into the house, in a pasture*, and *of brick* are called **phrases.**

2. These **phrases** may express *time, place,* or *manner.*

Time: *In the morning* the boys broke camp.
Place: The tree grew *near the house.*
Manner: The girls worked *without stopping.*

3. Think of phrases showing place that might be used in these sentences. Example: *in a valley.*

    1. The soldiers camped ———.   2. The bear slept ———.

3. The pirates hid their gold ———.   5. The boys swam ———.
4. The ship came to anchor ———.

4. Think of several phrases showing time that might be used in each of these sentences.   Example: *before daylight*.

The men returned home ———.   The plant blossomed ———.
The baby awoke ———.   The children played ———.
——— the boys coasted.   ——— the girls read stories.

5. Think of several phrases showing manner that might be used in these sentences.   Example: *with heads erect*.

The girls walked ———.   The angry woman answered ———.
The boy fought the fire ———.   The lazy dog moved ———.
The men spoke ———.

6. Using Words Correctly

Test L. First Form. Using Adjectives and Adverbs Correctly

Complete each of the following comparisons, using a form of one of the words given below Number 5:

1. The waterfall was the ——— one we had seen.
2. Of the two streams the one flowing south was the ———.
3. Of all the children Ruth was the ———.
4. Of the two brothers Henry is the ———.
5. Of the two cousins Margaret was the ———.

beautiful   narrow   lively   thoughtful   tall

Decide whether an adjective or an adverb should be put in each blank; then, with the help of the words below Number 10, copy and complete the sentences.

6. The boys ran ———.
7. The girls did their work ———.
8. The queen looked ———.
9. The old bear moved ——— than the young one.
10. The children did their work ———well.

swift   good   beautiful   clumsier   real
swiftly   well   beautifully   more clumsily   really

Chapter VIII — USEFUL OCCUPATIONS

1. Doing Useful Work

[Making pictures with words]

1. Add one or two sentences to each description, thus showing that you know what workmen are meant:

a. With spikes in his shoes, and a strap to hold him in place, a man works with wires at the top of a high pole. He wears gloves to protect himself from danger.

b. High in the air in the midst of noisy hammering men are working on a large steel frame. One man is heating rivets red hot and another is boring holes.

c. Wheels hum. Rods click. A workman is busy tending a machine which is using yarn wound on spindles and making it into cloth.

2. Think of some work that you have seen done in a kitchen, a shop, a factory, a creamery, a dairy, a telegraph office, or in some other place. Without naming your subject, give a description two or three sentences in length, and then ask your classmates to guess what you had in mind.

[Planning an investigation]

3. Name work done in your community about which you would like to be better informed; then volunteer to find the information asked for by some one in your class.

4. Be ready to give a report in the lesson on page 246

2. Building

[Conversation]

1. Accompanying the rat-tat of the hammer and the sound of the saw and plane, the carpenter whistles as he works. His life is a wholesome one and his work useful.

2. Tell your class in a sentence or two what use you yourself have made of tools, or what has interested you as you have watched builders at work.

3. In putting up a frame for a building, carpenters lay heavy timbers, or sills, on the foundation wall; they fit the floor joists into these sills, and then the pieces of studding which form the upright frame for the walls. Tell, if you can, what they use in the frame of the roof.

4. Point out in the drawing (a) the sills, (b) the

floor joists, (c) the studding, (d) the braces, (e) the rafters, and (f) the ridgepole.   Define each part by telling for what it is used.

5. Complete the following outline:

Putting up a Frame for a Building

I. Material used: heavy timber for sills and floor joists; lighter timber for studding, braces, rafters, and ridgepole.

II. The order in which the work is done: ———, ———, ———, ———, ———, ———, ———.

6. In putting up a building of concrete, what materials does a mason use?   What order does he follow in doing the work?

[Making an explanation clear]

7. Tell why in giving an explanation you should arrange the facts in order.   In what way does an outline help?

8. Use one of these suggestions to help you in planning a talk:

a. Tell the story of an experience that you have had (1) in using tools or (2) in watching a carpenter.

b. Describe a home that you would like to build. Begin by saying, If I could build a house just as I wished, I should first of all ———.

c. With the help of the outline in Exercise 5, explain how carpenters put up the frame of a building.

d. Explain how building is done with concrete or with brick.   First think out an outline like the one in Exercise 5.

e. By observing freight and by asking questions, find out the places from which the building material in your locality comes.   Make a report to your class.

Before giving your paper, read the suggestions given on page 289.

Before giving your paper, read the suggestions given on page 289.

[Vocabulary study — Adverbs]

9. Complete, using a different adverb in each sentence:

The carpenters worked ———.   They laid the sills ———.
They used their tools ———.   They fitted each joint ———.

10. Use adverbs in other sentences telling about the work done by carpenters.

3. Making the World " Brighter "

I

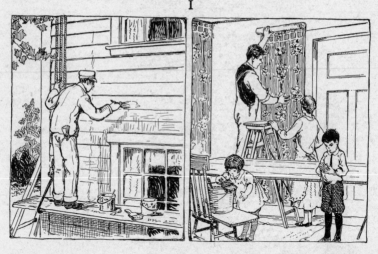

[Conversation]

1. Back and forth a house painter wields his brush and a surface discolored with dirt comes out looking fresh and clean. What change is wrought by a paper hanger?

2. What are some of the things that you have

noticed about a painter and his work. About a paper hanger and his work?

[Using an outline]

3. Supply the missing items in this outline:

I. The paper hanger's equipment: overalls to protect his clothes, board and standards, shears and brushes, stepladder, paper, and paste.

II. Order of work: cutting paper the right length, trimming edges, pasting and folding paper, matching the pattern in hanging the paper, using a stiff brush to smooth out the air bubbles and wrinkles, cutting off extra lengths.

III. The success of the work dependent upon care in preparing the wall, ———, ———, ———.

4. With the help of your class write on the board an outline for a talk on a painter's work.

5. Make suggestions for an outline for talks on cleaning silver. On washing windows. On scrubbing a floor.

6. In preparing a report to your class, choose a, b, or c:

a. Prepare a talk using the outline in Exercise 3.

b. Use the outline on the board and give a talk on painting.

c. Plan a report on calcimining, whitewashing, painting screens, washing windows, cleaning silver, scrubbing a floor, or some other form of work with which you have helped or about which you have some information.

[Giving a talk]

7. With the help of an outline get your talk well in mind before you try to give it.

[Written composition]

8. Make sure that you can write the words used in your talk, and then, after deciding how you can improve it, write the talk.

9. Why should a paper based on the outline in Exercise 3 be written in three paragraphs? In how many paragraphs should your own paper be written?

II

[Vocabulary study — Adverbs]

10. Complete, using a different adverb in each sentence, and name the word which the adverb modifies:

1. The men began their work ———.
2. They cleaned the walls ———.
3. They did their cutting ———.
4. They hung the paper ———.
5. They matched the pattern ———.
6. They tried ——— hard to keep the paper clean.
7. They worked ——— until five o'clock.
8. They left ———.
9. The work was done ———.

11. Proof-read your paper (see Exercise 8) first for paragraphing and then for spelling and for the correct use of adverbs.

4. Local Industries

[Oral and written composition]

1. In carrying out the plan made on page 241, be ready to include work done in the homes as well as that done on the farm, in shops, in factories and elsewhere. Before giving your talk, see that you

have a simple outline in mind, and that you have, if possible, samples of material and pictures to show.

2. After giving your talk and listening to the comments by the class, try to improve it so that it would be worth including in a booklet of industries made by your class.

5. Heroic Workmen

[Learning to study]

1. The building of our great irrigation dams, tunnels, and bridges has required heroic effort on the part of engineers and their workmen. Just what fortitude these men have shown is illustrated in the story of Gunnison Tunnel.

2. In order to get water to irrigate many thousands of acres in southwestern Colorado, men had to enter the Black Canyon of the Gunnison River, which every one had pronounced impenetrable and from which even the Indians who had entered it had never returned. In spite of this an engineer by the name of Torrence and four men had themselves lowered by ropes into the canyon. For three weeks the men climbed, and waded and swam, fighting exhaustion, fatigue, the icy river, and other obstacles in the dark canyon. At the end of that time they reached a place which they named the Falls of Sorrow, for here they despaired of ever making their escape. Their leader, however, finally discovered the bed of a watercourse leading precipitously into the canyon twenty-five hundred feet above them. The following story tells what happened:

A DIZZY CLIMB

When morning came the men started upward. Tied to a common rope and armed with spikes, they ascended one after another; Torrence led, each man making a firm foothold, and hauling in the slack or cautiously paying out rope in case of a sudden slip. At a snail's pace they gingerly picked their way, the greatest danger being that those above might loosen stones that would crash down upon those coming after.

By noon the men clung to the precipice like flies. From beneath them a thousand dizzy feet came the note of the white-churned stream. Above them, a towering fifteen hundred feet, arched the blue sky. In their veins was the fever of excitement, and in their hearts the sickening dread that the leader would announce that the course terminated impassably in a vertical wall of smooth rock. But still the men pressed on, buoyed by the nervous energy of those who fight for life.

Two thousand feet up, within five hundred feet of the top, night closed in. It found the climbers in a dreadful plight. Their hands were cut, their throats parched, their eyes blood-shot and their faces covered with a quarter-inch-thick mask where a layer of rock dust had settled and had been baked in with perspiration.

To spend the night clinging to the side of a precipice, within five hundred feet of their goal, was more than could be expected of human fortitude. The men therefore decided to take a chance on groping their way in the dark. For five hours they proceeded until, with a shout, Torrence grasped the stem of an overhanging sagebrush, and pulled himself clear of the canyon.

Panting, dripping with perspiration, one after another of the men climbed on to the brink and on hands and knees crawled to safety.

3. Tell what impressed you most about the story.

4. What idea do you gain from each of the following words in italics?

>At a snail's pace the men *gingerly* picked their way.
>They feared that the leader would announce that the course *terminated* impassably in a *vertical* wall.
>The men pressed on *buoyed* by the nervous energy of those who fight for life.
>Their throats were *parched*.
>They decided to take a chance on *groping* their way in the dark.
>The men climbed to the *brink* of the canyon.

5. The first paragraph in the story tells about the morning climb. Find the topic for each of the other paragraphs.

6. What opportunity to show heroism does a bridge-builder sometimes have?

7. Name opportunities to show heroism met by a miner; a railway engineer; a wireless operator; a sailor; a fireman.

[Using an outline in giving a talk]

8. With the help of one of these suggestions prepare a talk to give to your class.

>a. Tell the story of *A Dizzy Climb* as Torrence the leader might have told it.
>b. Give a talk beginning with these words:
>>Workmen as well as soldiers have many opportunities of showing heroism.
>c. Tell a true story of the heroism of a fireman, the captain of a ship, a railway engineer, or of some other man following a career that requires bravery.
>d. Imagine yourself trapped in a mine, in a sinking ship, in a burning building, or in some other dangerous situation. Tell of your escape.

Before giving your talk, see that you have an out-line of it well in mind and that you put in practice other things that you have learned this year about making a talk a success.

6. Review and Summary

I. Pronunciation and Meaning of Words

1. Show that you can pronounce each of the fol-lowing words distinctly and that you can use it cor-rectly in a sentence:

factory (fac to ry)	equipment (e quip ment)
machinery (ma chin er y)	automobile (au to mo bile)
studding (stud ding)	engineer (en gi neer)
joist (joist)	industry (in dus try)
material (ma te ri al)	precipice (prec i pice)
calcimining (cal ci min ing)	precipitous (pre cip i tous)

2. Hold a pronunciation contest using the words on pages 157, 177, 192, 207, 220, and 234.

II. Preparing a Paper to Keep

3. To complete the set of papers that you are to bind together as a record of your year's work in composition, choose the paper written in the lesson on page 244, or write the talk that you gave in the lesson on page 242 or in the one on page 247.

4. Proof-read your paper with the suggestions on page 292 in mind; copy it if necessary, and then bind it with the other papers that you have saved during the year.

5. Compare your first papers with the last ones

and try to get an idea of how much you have improved in your work.   Keep in mind the points given in the score on page 295.

7. The Parts of a Sentence

I. Subject and Predicate

1. In expressing a thought, we must have something to talk about and something to say of it.   In saying, *The sun is shining*, we are speaking of *the sun;* what we say of it is that it *is shining*.

2. The part of a sentence of which something is said is called the **subject.**

The sun | is shining
subject

3. Give sentences using the following words as subjects:

Engineers	The city of Washington
Firemen	New York City
Miners	Fast steamers
Sailors	Fast trains

4. The part of a sentence that says something of the subject is called the **predicate.**

The sun | is shining
predicate

5. Supply a subject for each predicate:

——— grows in the south.	——— are fierce animals.
——— is a high mountain.	——— is a bird of prey.
——— is a large river.	——— makes a faithful friend.
——— live in the north.	——— grow to be very large.

6. Find the predicate that goes with each subject:

Subjects	Predicates
The United States	win success
The President	is a large country
Teachers	governs the country
Boys of strong character	win many friends
Girls with gentle manners	govern a school

7. Tell which is missing, the subject or the predicate; then supply it:

1. ran away
2. was careful
3. the boy's mother
4. drew a picture
5. fairy stories
6. wild flowers
7. cried aloud
8. the mother bird
9. lay asleep
10. woke with a start
11. built our school
12. the telephone
13. did an errand
14. knocked at the door
15. the cattle in the field
16. a new automobile

8. Name the subject and the predicate of each of these sentences:

1. The boys went fishing.
2. The elephant lifted his trunk.
3. The dog barked fiercely.
4. The flowers in the garden are in blossom.
5. The child played with his toys.

II. Placing of the Subject and the Predicate

1. To make a thought more emphatic, the order of words in a sentence is often changed. The sentence *Down came the airplane* sounds more exciting than *The airplane came down.*

2. In which of these sentences does the subject come first?

> Mary ran across the playground.
> Across the playground ran Mary.

3. Rearrange the parts of these sentences so that the subject comes first; then name for each sentence the subject and the predicate:

1. Down the street galloped the horse.
2. Above the clouds rose the aeroplane.
3. Across the fields ran the frightened cattle.
4. Up the ladder climbed the firemen.
5. Down the chimney came good St. Nick.

4. Give the subject and the predicate of each of these sentences; then arrange the words so that the subject comes last:

1. The sailor leaped overboard.
2. The burglar jumped out of the window.
3. The hawk flew away with the little chick.
4. The boy jumped into the boat.
5. The boat sailed slowly down the river.

5. Arrange the words in each sentence so that the subject comes first, if they are not already so arranged; then give the subject and the predicate of each sentence:

1. Into the woods ran the fox.
2. In the bushes hid the little rabbit.
3. Down the street ran the boy.
4. On the mountain top burned a signal fire.
5. Violets grew in the deep woods.
6. Into the water leaped the frogs.
7. The farmer ploughed his field.
8. The woman was baking bread.

9. "Look out," shouted the boys.
10. A growl came from a cave.
11. Around the fire danced the Indians.
12. "Shoulder guns," commanded the officer.
13. The street musician played his organ.
14. The monkey begged for pennies.
15. Across the yard ran the children pell-mell.
16. The old woman carried a bundle on her head.
17. The boys rode their bicycles along the country road.
18. Overhead an airplane was sailing.
19. Down the mountain side roared a waterfall.
20. Into the river plunged the frightened deer.

III. Combining Ideas in a Sentence

1. Our thoughts are often of a character that may be expressed in a statement made up of a single subject and predicate. At other times they require more than one subject or predicate.

2. Read these sentences. How many subjects has the first sentence? How many predicates has the second sentence?

Lilacs, snowballs, and iris were in bloom.
The bird darted from its nest and flew away.

When a sentence has two or more subjects, the subject is **compound.**

3. What is meant by a compound predicate?

4. Tell which of these sentences have compound subjects and which have compound predicates:

1. Horses and cattle were feeding in the pasture.
2. The rivers, lakes, and ponds were frozen.
3. Father sent a telegram and wrote a letter.

4. Down the hill ran the boys and girls.

5. The boys shouted and ran.

6. The girls danced and sang.

7. The car went rapidly down the street and turned the corner.

8. In the tree tops robins and catbirds built their nests.

9. In the swamp lived heron and wild duck.

10. The partridge flew to the stump and drummed with his wings.

11. The loon screamed and then disappeared beneath the water.

12. In the deep woods foxes and bears made their dens.

13. Under the brush rabbits made their homes and raised their young.

14. Frogs and turtles could be seen on the shore of the pond.

15. The old grizzly and her cubs left her den and wandered through the woods.

16. The boys and their friends tramped through the woods and fished in the brooks.

5. Give illustrations of your own to show that you understand these definitions:

The subject of a sentence is that of which something is said. Ex. *The bird in the tree* was singing gayly.

The predicate of a sentence is that which is said of the subject. Ex. The bird in the tree *was singing gayly*.

The subject of a sentence is compound when in a single statement the verb has more than one subject. Ex. *Robins* and *bluebirds* were the first to arrive.

The predicate of a sentence is compound when in a single statement there is more than one verb. Ex. The plants *blossomed* and then *went* to seed.

A sentence is in its natural order when the subject comes first. Ex. The ship sailed down the river.

Optional Exercises: The Conjunction

In combining words and statements, we use words that are "joining" words. We may say, "John *and* Mary went to the picnic," "Helen *or* Ruth is to stay at home," "You may go *if* you wish to."

Words like *and*, *or*, and *if* are called **conjunctions**.

A conjunction is a word used to connect words or groups of words.

Give other sentences in which you use the conjunctions in italics:

1. Gold *and* silver are precious metals.
2. The boy is trustworthy *although* he is slow.
3. Frank is an old friend; *therefore* I can trust him.
4. My brother is going, *but* I shall stay at home.

Complete, using the conjunctions *so that, if, for, so, but, although*:

6. He will go ——— he can get permission.
7. John was ashamed, ——— he would not own it.
8. Mary bought sugar, ——— she was planning to make candy.
9. Helen is ready for the high school, ——— she is only eleven years old.
10. Fred was tired ——— he went to bed early.

Combine, using such conjunctions as, *and, or, but, if, although, since, therefore, so that*:

1. John went to school. His brother went to school.
2. Helen went to church. Helen went to Sunday School.
3. Tom went on a trip. His brother stayed at home.
4. Ruth will go to school. Ruth will stay at home.
5. Henry is going. Henry is ready for high school.
6. It is late. We must start.
7. The fire whistle blew twice. We knew the fire was out.
8. The boy apologized. I forgave him.
9. It was late in the spring. The weather was cold. There was ice on the ponds.

8. Summary — The Parts of Speech

1. There are eight kinds of words or parts of speech. The five which you have studied are all represented in the following sentence:

The	brave	soldier	carried	his	gun	proudly
adjective	adjective	noun	verb	pronoun	noun	adverb

2. Make sure that you understand the following definitions and can give other examples of each part of speech.

A noun is a name of a person, place, or thing.   Ex. *bird, John, earth, goodness.*

A pronoun is a word used in place of a noun.   Ex. *he, it, they, our, who, yourself.*

A verb is a word used to assert action or being.   Ex. *runs, remember, is, seems.*

An adjective is a word used to modify the meaning of a noun or pronoun.   Ex. *young, pretty, faithful.*

An adverb is a word used to modify the meaning of a verb, an adjective, or another adverb.   Ex. *swiftly, carefully, westward, early, very, really, too.*

3. What part of speech is each word in the following sentences?

1. Hurry!
2. Clouds gathered.
3. The wind blew.
4. A heavy rain fell.
5. The boy ran swiftly.
6. John lost his hat.
7. A train whistled.
8. I stopped my car.
9. The man was careful.
10. The steamboat traveled slowly.
11. The engine pulled a heavy load.
12. The farmer's horse ran away.
13. The hay wagon fell over.
14. The carpenter built a large hall.
15. The mason made the chimney.
16. The truck carried a heavy load.

Optional Work

The three parts of speech you will learn to know better another year are (1) words like *and* and *but* used to join other words; (2) words like *on, of, for, from,* used to introduce such phrases as *on a tree, of gold, for his mother, from a distance;* (3) words like *oh, pshaw, alas, hurrah.*

Words like *and* and *but* are called **conjunctions.**   (See page 256.)

A conjunction is a word used to connect words or groups of words.

Words like *on, of, for, from* are **prepositions.**

A preposition is a word used to show relation.

Words like *oh, pshaw, alas, hurrah* are **interjections.**

An interjection is a word used as an exclamation.

9. Mastery of the Sentence. Test No. 3

Copy the groups of words that form complete sentences: /o

1. The sun rose behind a cloud
2. Far away from the house
3. The hawk flying overhead
4. Before the flowers were in bloom
5. The bird which was hungry captured the worm
6. Now the maid who was milking the cow no sooner heard some one speak than she recognized the voice as that
7. Out in the yard in the midst of the garden and brier patch was a fountain which was made of marble .

Find the ends of the sentences; then copy the exercises, putting in the capitals and periods that are needed:

8. Be orderly about your work do not waste anything never be idle when you decide to do anything do it with a brave heart.
9. Bright sunlight flooded the swamp everything seemed soaking in the warm light a little brown sparrow teetered above a pool of water on a long rush a turtle sunned itself on a tuft of grass.

Copy the following sentences, inserting in each the marks of punctuation needed to make the thought clear:

10. The World War ended with the signing of the Armistice November 11 1918
11. The ship carried a cargo of flour fruit and other food
12. Why should you be afraid asked the sailor
13. Father speak louder cried the boy I cannot hear what you say

Combine the sentences in each exercise so that

they will form one clear sentence: you may omit words and add others, but you must not change the thought:

14. Mary is good in music. She is not good in drawing.
15. When spring came the wild geese flew north. The wild ducks flew north, too.
16. The river was narrow at one place. The bridge crossed it at this place.
17. Some of the boys were on the ball team. These boys went to the grounds early. The others went later.

Compare your record with the following standards. If it is unsatisfactory, try to improve it.

Standard score: *Fair*, 9–10 correct exercises; *good*, 11–12 correct exercises; *excellent*, 13–17 correct exercises.

10. Writing Letters

I. A Letter of Application

1. With the help of the following letter show that you can write in good form a letter applying for work during the summer. Give information concerning your education and experience and also references that would help the company in learning about you.

640 Jersey St., Quincy, Ill.
June 14, 1928

R. A. Day Company
  112 East Fourth St.
      Quincy, Ill.
Gentlemen:
      In answer to your advertisement in the Daily News of June 13, I wish to apply for the position of errand boy. I am fifteen years of age. Last summer

I worked as a delivery boy for Woodman Brothers, 11 Willow Avenue. For information about me I have permission to refer you to Woodman Brothers, to Mr. E. M. Davis, principal of the Henry Clay School, and to Mr. Henry Johnson, Scout Master, 40 Pine Street.

Yours very truly,

John Robinson

Make your letter a reply to an advertisement found in a newspaper or to one of the following notices:

Wanted. A boy under 18 years, to learn the grocery business. Apply by letter to Egan's Market, 18 Central Street.

Girls wanted to make artificial flowers; pleasant work. Write to M. E. Morgan, 357 Third Avenue. All applicants should give references.

II. A Letter of Appreciation

In order to show your appreciation of all that your teacher has done for you, you might write her a note telling her what you have enjoyed most during the year, and thanking her for all the trouble she has taken for you. Put the letter in an envelope. Address the envelope properly and either send the letter through the mail or lay it on your teacher's desk.

11. Using Words Correctly. Review for the Second Half Year

Test J. Second Form. Speaking of One or More

Copy and complete, using words from below Number 5:

1. One of the best players ——— unable to play.
2. Crowds of people ——— going to the game.
3. Every one of the seats ——— taken.
4. Neither of the books ——— been returned.
5. ——— the tickets ready?

is	is	was	has	wasn't
are	are	were	have	weren't

Use words from the list below Number 10 in completing these sentences:

6. ——— Tom wish to go?
7. ——— the leader arrived?
8. Not one of the days ——— cloudy.
9. Each of the games ——— been exciting.
10. The boys in the class ——— all there.

doesn't	haven't	was	has	was
don't	hasn't	were	have	were

Test K. Second Form. Avoiding Senseless Expressions

Copy and complete, using words from below Number 4:

1. If I had had permission I ——— gone.
2. The strip of leather made ——— strap.
3. My brother ——— yet.
4. Mary sings ——— she enjoyed it.

should a	a sort of	has not gone	like
should have	a sort of a	did not go	as if

Use words from below Number 8 to complete these sentences:

5. The boys ——— to walk across the lawn.
6. They should ——— better.
7. With the help of a pulley the piano was ———.
8. The men were asked to ———.

ought not	of known	elevated	take hold
hadn't ought	have known	elevated up	take a hold

Test L. Second Form. Using Adjectives and Adverbs Correctly

Copy and complete each sentence, using a form of one of the words given below Number 5:

1. The task was the ――― one that the boys had undertaken.
2. Of the two brothers Henry is the ――― driver.
3. Of all the highways in the United States the Columbia Highway is the ―――.
4. The mountains in the west are ――― than those in the east.
5. Of the two rivers the Missouri is the ―――.

difficult   careful   beautiful   high   long

Use words from below Number 10 in completing these sentences:

6. The lion roared ―――.
7. The traveler looked ―――.
8. The boy played ball ―――.
9. The older men worked ――― than the young men.
10. I am feeling ―――, thank you.

fierce   weary   well   steadier   fine
fiercely   wearily   good   more steadily   finely

Better English Club Report

In completing the work of the half year, be ready to applaud those in the class who have made the finest record on the tests, and also to give a vote of thanks to the president of your club, the club counselor, and the poster committee for all the work that they have done to help the club in acquiring the habit of using better English.

Chapter IX — A GUIDE TO CORRECT USAGE
Use of Guide

The exercises in this guide are to help you in correcting the errors that you sometimes make in your everyday speech. Use the tests throughout the book to find out what errors you need to correct and the guide to help you in mastering the right expressions.

Test A.   Practice Exercises.   Common Errors

1. **Saw, have seen; did, have done; came, have come.**[1] Say:

> I **saw** a hawk.   I **have seen** a hawk.
> Father **came** home early.   Father **has come** home.
> The man **did** his work.   The man **has done** his work.

[1] For poster suggestions see the footnote on page 264.

Saw, *did*, and *came* are used without a helping word. *Seen*, *come*, and *done* are used with such helping words as *have*, *has*, *had*, *is*, *are*, *was*, and *were*.[1]

a. Think of facts that you have learned in geography and then write at least seven sentences like the following:

> I *came* from the South where I *saw* cotton growing.
> I *came* from Japan where I *saw* cherry trees in bloom.

b. Answer these questions using the word *did:*

> Where did you do your studying last evening?
> With whom did you do your work?
> When did you do your arithmetic problems?
> When did you do your spelling lesson?

c. Find in the stories in this book, or elsewhere, sentences that show how *saw*, *did*, and *came* are used. Write the sentences to help you in mastering the correct use of the words.[2]

d. Write three pairs of sentences of your own like each of those in Exercise 1, page 263.

[1] *Poster suggestion:* Select one of the following rhymes or a similar one containing words with which the class needs help. Draw a picture illustrating it, and then print the rhyme below the picture.

> "I *saw* a robin sitting in a tree
> Up went pussy and down *came* he."
>
> I *did* my work.   Now that it's *done*
> Let's laugh and play and have some fun.
>
> When the boys *came* out to play,
> Georgie Porgie *ran* away.
>
> The maid was in the garden hanging out the clothes
> When down *came* a blackbird and nipped off her nose.

[2] For games requiring the use of these words, see *The Open Door Language Series, First Book*, pages 8, 20, 139.

2. **Ran, have run.** Say:

> The boys **ran** a race.   The boys **have run** a race.
> Do not use *run* for *ran*.

a. Give pairs of sentences showing how to use *ran* and *have run* or *has run*.

> Ex.: The girls *ran* home.   The girls *have run* home.

b. Make up stories like the following in which you tell of escaping from danger by running:

> (1) When I was climbing a mountain, a bear chased me.   I ran to the nearest tree.
> (2) When I was at a circus, a lion escaped from its cage and chased me.   I ran for the entrance.
> (3) When I was on a farm, a cow chased me.   I ran for the nearest fence.

c. Write at least seven sentences showing the correct use of *ran*.

3. **Have** and **got.** Say:

> I **have** a book.   I **got** it from the shelf.
> The word *got* means *obtained* and not *possessed*.   It should not be used in such sentences as *I have a bicycle* or *I haven't a bicycle*.

a. Give other pairs of sentences like the following:

> We have a radio set.   We got it from a dealer in New York.
> I have my cloak.   I got it from the closet.
> Do not use *got* where it is not needed.   Do not say I *haven't got any.*

b. Be ready to play this game or one of your own like it:

> Game. Corner Grocery. Each player writes on a slip of paper the name of some article found in a grocery story, such as sugar, butter, rice, flour, or crackers. The players exchange slips and the leader tries to guess what each has. He may ask a player, "Have you sugar?" The player must answer by saying, "Yes, I have some" or "I haven't any." The leader asks ten questions and then chooses some one to take his place. The number of correct guesses is kept as his score.

4. **Haven't.**[1] Say:

| I **haven't** any. | I **haven't** a book. |
| I **have** none. | I **have** no book. |

Do not use in the same statement two words that mean *not*. To say that *I haven't none* is the same as to say *I have not none* which means *I have some*. To say *I haven't no book* is the same as to say *I have one or more books*.

a. Complete:

(1) A bat has wings, but it ——— feathers.

(2) A mole can find its way, but it ——— eyes.

(3) Young robins have speckled breasts, but old robins ———.

(4) The male humming bird has gay plumage, but the female ———.

(5) Eagles have strong beaks and talons but birds that feed upon seeds ———.

b. Write at least five other sentences like those in Exercise a:

---

[1] For games see *The Open Door Language Series, First Book*, pages 8, 36, 272.

5. **He, she,** and **I.** Say:

I am going.   My sister and **I** went.   **He and she** were there.

(1) In making statements about persons, use *he*, *she*, and *I*.   Do not say, *John and me are going*, or *Him and her were there*. (2) When speaking of yourself and some one else at the same time, remember to name the other person first.   If you say *I and John*, it looks as if you thought more of yourself than of him.   Say *John and I*.

a. Write a puzzle like the following one. Begin each statement with *He and I* or with *She and I*.

OF WHOM AM I THINKING?

He and I are in the same class.
He and I have a combined age of twenty.
He and I are on the same ball team.
He and I live on the same street.
He and I walk to school together.

b. Give your puzzle to some one to guess.

c. Write five other sentences showing the use of *he*, *she*, and *I*.

6. **It was he, she, we,** or **they.** Say:

It was he whom you saw.
It was she who helped you.
It was I who knocked.
It was we who left.
It was they who came early.

Use *he*, *she*, *I*, and *they* after the words *it is* and *it was*.

a. Give sentences of your own like those above, and then be ready to play the following game or a similar one made up by yourselves.

Game.   WHO TOOK IT?   The leader is sent
from the room.   While he is gone, one player takes
a book from the teacher's desk and gives it to
another player, who places it on the leader's desk.
When the leader returns, he tries to tell by the
expression of the faces who were the ones that
touched the book.   He takes the players in turn
and asks such questions as "Was it Henry who
took the book?"   The player answers, "It was he"
or "It was not he."   After finding out who took
the book, he asks, "Was it Mary who put the
book on my desk?"   The player answers, "It
was she" or "It was not she."

b. Write three or more sentences containing
it was he; three containing *it was she;* and
three containing *it was I.*

Test B.   Practice Exercises.   Giving Words their Right Meaning

In doing any one of the following exercises, first
give several sentences of your own showing the correct use of the words printed in heavy black type;
then complete the sentences containing blanks.

1. **Bring, take.**   Say:

Bring the new books to me and **take** the old ones away.

A person may use the word *bring* when the action is toward him. He should not use it when the action is away from him.

(1) Tom's mother asked him to take the ashes to the cellar and to ———— her some coal.

(2) Mary's teacher asked her to ———— her book home with her and to ———— it to school in the morning.

2. Good, well. Say:

The boy is a **good** penman.   He writes **well**.

Use *good* to describe a person or thing, but not an action.   Do not say a person *writes good*.

(1) Margaret is a *good* singer.   She sings ————.
(2) Tom is a *good* baseball player.   He plays ————.
(3) Fred swims ————.
(4) Ruth plays a piano ————.
(5) Henry is a *good* reader.   He reads ————.

3. Leave, let. Say:

Leave your book on your desk.   **Let** me have your pencil, please.

Leave means *to let alone*.   *Let* means to *allow* or *permit*.   Do not use *leave* in asking permission or at any other time when *let* should be used.

(1) Sometimes I *leave* my bicycle on the porch, but mother never ———— me put it in the hall.

(2) Father never ———— me play in the street.

(3) Mother ———— me visit my grandmother.

4. Lie, lay.[1] Say:

Lay the book on the table and let it **lie** there.

In commands like that above the word *lay* is followed

[1] *Poster suggestion:* The following rhyme may be copied and illustrated:

> Hush-a-bye, baby, *lie* still with thy daddy,
>   Thy mammy *has gone* to the mill
> To get some meal to bake a cake,
>   So pray, my dear baby, *lie* still.

by the name of an object such as book, pencil, or desk.
The word *lie* is not followed by the name of an object.
You cannot *lie* anything.

(1) Mother (to a child): *Lay* your pillow down and then ——— down and go to sleep.

(2) Father (to a boy): ——— the tools in the drawer.

(3) Nurse (to a baby): ——— down in your crib.

(4) Girl (to her kitten): ——— still and let me stroke you.

(5) Boy (to his dog): ——— the bone down and then ——— by the door.

(6) Woman (to a tired guest) ——— your hat on the table and then ——— down for a rest.

5. **May, can.** Say:

May I go home, please? **Can** Tom swim?

In asking permission, use *may;* in asking whether an action is possible or not, use the word *can*. Do not use *can* for *may*.

(1) Tom *can* skate. ——— he go skating with me, please?

(2) Mary *can* row. ——— she use your boat, please?

(3) I *can* walk fast. ——— I go to walk with you?

(4) I *can* cook. ——— I make some candy for you?

Tests C, F, and I. Practice Exercises. Telling What Happened

The following words are sometimes incorrectly used. Each has three forms, or parts, called its principal parts. The first part is used to express present time. The second part is used to denote past time and may be used with *yesterday, this morn-ing, last week*. The third is used with *have, has*, or *had*, and also with *is, are, was,* or *were*.   It is correct to say:

> I *sing* a song every morning.   Yesterday I *sang* a hymn.   I *have sung* many kinds of songs.

The principal parts of *sing* are *sing, sang, have sung*.

If in Tests C, F, or I, you made an error in the use of one of the following words, you are to learn the principal parts of the word and then practice giving sentences of your own showing how the second and third parts should be used.

1. **Begin, began, (have) begun.**   Yesterday I **began** taking music lessons.   I **have begun** taking music lessons.

2. **Blow, blew, (have) blown.**   The wind **blew** a hurricane.   The wind **has blown** a hurricane.

3. **Break, broke, (have) broken.**   The window **broke.** The window **was broken.**

4. **Come, came, (have) come.**   The girl's aunt **came** to visit her.   The girl's aunt **has come** to visit her.

5. **Choose, chose, (have) chosen.**   The team **chose** a leader.   The team **has chosen** a leader.

6. **Do, did, (have) done.**   Fred **did** his work well. Fred **has done** his work well.

7. **Draw, drew, (have) drawn.**   I **drew** a map.   I **have drawn** a map.

8. **Drown, drowned, (have) drowned.**   The kittens **drowned.**   The kittens **were drowned.**
    Drowned is pronounced as one syllable.

9. **Drink, drank, (have) drunk.**   The horses **drank** from the brook.   The horses **have drunk** from the brook.

10. **Eat, ate, (have) eaten.**   Thanksgiving I **ate** some turkey.   I **have eaten** turkey.

11. **Freeze, froze, (have) frozen.**   On his birthday Tom **froze** some ice cream.   Tom **has frozen** some ice cream.

12. **Go, went, (have) gone.**   Father **went** to work early.   Father **has gone** to work.

13. **Give, gave, (have) given.**   I **gave** my brother a present.   I **have given** my brother a present.

14. **Lie, lay, (have) lain.**[1]   The dog **lay** by the fire. The dog **has lain** by the fire.

15. **Lay, laid, (have) laid.**   The boy **laid** the book on the shelf.   The boy **has laid** the book on the shelf.

16. **Ring, rang, (have) rung.**   The school bell **rang.** The school bell **has rung.**

17. **Rise, rose, (have) risen.**   The sun **rose.**   The sun has **risen.**

18. **Run, ran, (have) run.**   The boys **ran** a mile. The boys **have run** a mile.

19. **See, saw, (have) seen.**   The sailor **saw** a whale. The sailor **had seen** a whale.

20. **Set, set, (have) set.**   I **set** the table for dinner. I **have set** the table for dinner.

21. **Shake, shook, (have) shaken.**   Jane **shook** the rugs.   Jane **has shaken** the rugs.

22. **Sit, sat, (have) sat.**[1]   The woman **sat** on her door-step.   She **has sat** on her door-step.

23. **Sing, sang, (have) sung.**   The children **sang** a new song.   The children **have sung** a new song.

24. **Swim, swam, (have) swum.**   The scout **swam** across the stream.   He **has swum** across the stream.

25. **Swing, swung, (have) swung.**   The bird **swung** on a reed.   The bird **has swung** on a reed.

26. **Throw, threw, (have) thrown.**   The pitcher **threw** a curved ball.   The pitcher **has thrown** a ball.

27. **Write, wrote, (have) written.**   The boy **wrote** to his mother.   The boy **has written** to his mother.

---

[1] *Poster suggestions:* The following rhymes may be illustrated and used for posters to remind the class of the correct way of using the words printed in heavy black type:

This is the rat
That **ate** the malt
That **lay** in the house that
Jack Built.

Little Miss Muffet
Sat on a tuffet
Eating curds and whey.

Use these rhymes to help you in remembering the correct use of the words printed in heavy type; then plan a poster of your own. (See the footnote on page 272 for suggestions.)

> A·little·boy·
> went·into·a·barn
> And·**lay**·down·
> on·some·hay
> An·owl·**came**·
> out·and·**flew**·
> about·
> And·the·little·
> boy·**ran**·away

> MISTER·EAST·*GAVE*·A·FEAST
> MISTER·NORTH·*LAID*·THE·CLOTH·
> MISTER·WEST·*DID*·HIS·BEST·
> MISTER·SOUTH·*BURNT*·HIS·MOUTH·
> EATING·COLD·POTATO·

Game. FOLLOW THE LEADER.[1] The players close their books. The leader reads from page 271 or 272 a sentence containing a word that troubles the class. The player called upon must give the same sentence, using *have* or *has* with the correct form of the word given in the sentence. If the leader says, "The pitcher threw a curved ball," the player says, "The pitcher has thrown a curved ball." The leader then gives sentences to the other players in turn. Any one making a mistake must pay a forfeit determined by the class.

---

[1] For the games I DID IT, and MISSING WORD see *The Open Door Language Series, First Book*, pages 52 and 280.

Contest. The class chooses sides. The leaders take turns in calling for the principal parts of the verbs in the list above. The leader on one side may ask a person on the opposite side to give the principal parts of *see*. If the player called upon cannot say *see, saw, have seen*, he takes his seat and the next player on the same side tries to give them. The leader on the other side may then call for the principal parts of *sing* or of some other word. The side left with the larger number standing wins the contest.

Test D. Practice Exercises. Speaking of One or More

I

1. **Is, are; was, were; has, have.** Say:

The **boy is** studying.   The **boys are** studying.
The **girl was** in earnest.   The **girls were** in earnest.
The **man has** work to do.   The **men have** work to do.

In speaking of one thing, use *is, was, has*.
In speaking of more than one, use *are, were, have*.

a. Change the following sentences so that the person or thing spoken of means more than one:

Ex.: A woman *was* at work.   Women *were* at work.

(1) A man was running an engine.
(2) A boy was helping him.
(3) The engine was out of order.
(4) A bird was flying overhead.
(5) A rabbit is hiding in the bushes.
(6) A hawk is watching them.
(7) The girl has a book.
(8) The baby has a toy.
(9) The woman has an umbrella.
(10) There is one pencil left.

(11) There was a dog in the yard.
(12) There has been a tree cut down.
(13) Isn't your brother going?
(14) Wasn't the lesson hard?
(15) Hasn't the boy left?
(16) The bird in the tree is singing.

b. Write the sentences composed in Exercise a; then use the exercises on pages 210–211.

2. **Am I not.**[1] Say:

Am I not to be promoted?   I am to go with you, mother.   **Am I not?**

Many boys and girls in trying to avoid the words *am I not* use an incorrect expression such as *ain't I* or *aren't I*.   There is no contraction for the words *am* and *not*.[2]

Write at least five pairs of sentences like these:

I am improving in my work.   Am I not?

3. **Doesn't.** Say:

Doesn't Mary live near you?   **Doesn't she** play with you?
Doesn't Tom belong to the ball team?   **Doesn't he** pitch for you?

The answer to the first question might be Mary *does*. It could never be Mary *do*.   For this reason *doesn't* and not *don't* is used in asking the question.

[1] Where the expression *am I not?* sounds unnatural, a pupil may avoid the negative and use such expressions as *Am I to be promoted?* or *Shall I be promoted?*

[2] *Poster suggestion:* To help the class avoid using the word *ain't*, you may copy and illustrate the following rhyme:

A fat little boy who said *ain't*
Fell into a can of red paint.
    And when he got out,
    He said with a shout:
"I'll say *isn't*, and *aren't*, and not *ain't!*"
    Adapted from the Course of Study, Decatur, Illinois.

a. Write several questions like the following, contrasting the use of *doesn't* and *don't:*

> Doesn't John go to school?   Don't John and his brother go to school?

b. Write several sentences, similar to the following, showing what a cautious boy or girl doesn't do.

> A cautious boy doesn't run in front of an oncoming train.

4. **Shall I?** Say:

> **Shall I** go?   **Shall we** go?
>
> In asking a question *shall*, not *will*, should be used with the words *I* and *we*.

a. In playing the game WARM or COLD,[1] the person who is It tries to find some object by asking questions like the following: *Shall I look in the cupboard?   Shall I look on the table?* Make out a list of questions that you might ask in looking for some object hidden in your schoolroom.

b. Write seven or eight questions that you might ask yourself in choosing what you would like to be when you are grown.   Write your questions in this form: *Shall I be a teacher? Shall I be a doctor?*

5. **Were you? Are you?**   Say:

> **Were you** at school?
> **Are you** and your brother going away?

[1] See *The Open Door Language Series, First Book,* page 100.

Remember to use *were* and *are*, and not *was* or *is*, with the word *you*.

Write at least seven statements and questions like the following:

You were at church.   Weren't you?
You and your mother are going to the concert.   Aren't you?

Test E.   Practice Exercises.   Words often Confused

I

Their, our, its.   *Their*, *our*, and *its* are often confused with other words that sound either exactly like them or somewhat like them.   Before studying the others, you are to make sure that you know how to write these three words.   It is correct to write:

The boys had **their** brother with them.
Our school building is large.
This garden is **ours;** that one is **theirs.**
The book had lost **its** cover.

The words *our*, *ours*, *their*, *theirs*, and *its* express ownership.   Remember never to use an apostrophe in them.   Try not to confuse them with other words.

a. Give sentences showing how to use each word.   Spell the words.   For example, say:

The girls left their books on their desks; t-h-e-i-r their.

b. Copy and complete answers to the following questions, filling each blank with *our*, *ours*, *their*, *theirs*, or *its*.

(1) Is the baseball Tom's and Henry's? It isn't ———.

(2) Is it yours and your sister's? It isn't ———.

(3) Whose football did the boys have? They had ——— own.

(4) What is wrong with that bird? ——— wing is broken.

II

1. **Their, there.** Say:

The pirates buried **their** gold in the sand and **there** it lay a hundred years.

Their shows ownership. *There* is used to show place. You can remember how to spell *there* by comparing it with *here*, which is also used to show place. Keep in mind the expression *here and there*. Remember also that if you drop the *t* from *there* you have *here*.

a. Use in sentences:

their cousins	there near the water
their friends	there in the orchard
their baseball	there in the sky
their rabbits	here and there in the field

b. Give sentences using both *their* and *there* in one sentence.

Illustration: The boys knew that several of *their* friends would be *there* to help them.

c. Complete, using *there* or *their:*

(1) The girls had ———— books with them.

(2) The trees grew ———— near the house.

(3) The boys hid ———— bicycles behind the trees.

(4) ———— were ten boys in the club.

(5) ———— were many presents on the Christmas tree.

(6) The children hung ———— stockings by the fireplace.

(7) Here and ———— and everywhere the children looked for ———— lost kitten.

2. Their, there, they. Say:

The girls that were **there** had **their** work baskets with them. **They** were busy sewing.

The word *they* refers to people or things. It rhymes with *say* and *may*. Do not confuse it with *their* and *there* which rhyme with *care* and *fare*.

Copy and complete Exercise c; then write at least six sentences of your own showing the correct use of *their*, *there*, and *they*.

3. Our, are. Say:

The plants in **our** garden **are** growing well.

The word *our* shows ownership (see page 277). It rhymes with *flour* and *sour*. Do not confuse it with *are* which rhymes with *star* and *car*.

Give five or more pairs of sentences of your own like the following:

Our school is a busy place. There *are* many children in it.

Our class studies hard. We *are* learning much that is useful.

Our long vacation comes in the summer. We *are* looking forward to it.

4. **Its, it's.**   Say:

It's (it is) too bad that the kitten hurt **its** paw.

Its shows ownership.   It is written without an apostrophe.   Do not confuse it with *it's*, which means *it is.*
Give sentences of your own like the following:
See the bird.   It's either too young to fly or it has broken its wing.
My rabbit is old.   It's too old to escape from the dogs.   Its legs are stiff.

5. **Two, to, too.**   Say:

Two of my brothers have gone **to** the city.   My sister went **too.**

Two means one and one more.   *To* means toward. *Too* means *also,* or it may answer the question *How much?* Of these three words the word *too* causes the most trouble.

a. Give other sentences like the following:

I have *two* pets.
I like *to* play with my cat.   I like *to* play with my dog *too.*
I am going *to* New York and *to* Washington *too.*
I spilt some water.   The cup was *too* full.

b. Decide which word (*to, too,* or *two*) can be used before each word given here:

—— play	—— full	—— stars	—— walk
—— laugh	—— many	—— trees	—— paths
—— run	—— small	—— write	—— rabbits
—— girls	—— jump	—— sing	—— low
—— boys	—— dogs	—— large	—— dance
—— cats	—— little	—— high	—— run

6. **New, knew.**   Say:

Our books were **new.** We **knew** our lessons.

Give at least five other sentences showing the difference in *new* and *knew*.

Test F. Practice Exercises. Telling what Happened

These exercises will be found on pages 270–274.

Test G. Practice Exercises. Twelve Common Errors

1. See pages 263–268 for the use of *saw, have seen; did, have done; came, have come; ran, have run; have, got; haven't; he, she, and I; it was he, she, I,* or *they.*

2. **Than I, we, he, she,** or **they.** Notice that the thought in the following sentences is the same.

> My sister is younger **than I.**
> My sister is younger **than I am.**

a. What word is understood at the end of each of the following sentences?

> Fred's brother is stronger than he.
> The boys' rivals were better players than they.

b. The word following *than* is the subject of a statement part of which is understood. For this reason we say *than I, than we, than he, than she,* or *than they.* We do not say *than me,* for to say *My sister is younger than me am* sounds absurd.

c. Prove that the word *he* is the correct one to use in this sentence:

> The boy's uncle was older than he.

d. Complete:

John's mother is wiser than ———.
Helen's sister is a better cook than ———.
My father is taller than ———.
The twins' cousin is younger than ———.

e. Copy and complete the sentences in Exercise d; then write others like them.

3. **For him, her, me, us,** or **them.** Say:

The book is **for him and her.** Letters came **to him and me.**
When father and mother were away, a package came **from them.**
After words like *for, to, from, with,* and *between,* use the words *him, her, me,* and *them.*

a. Use in sentences:

to him   between you and me
from her   for him and me
for them   with her and me
with us   against him and her

b. Write the sentences that you composed in Exercise a.

Test H. Practice Exercises. Giving Words their Right Meaning

Give sentences of your own to show how each word in heavy black type should be used; then complete the sentences containing blanks.

1. **Borrow, lend.** Say:

Will you **lend** me your knife? May I **borrow** a knife from you?

You *lend to* a person or *borrow from* him.   Never say
May I lend a pencil from you?

(1) I can *lend* money to you, but I shall have to
———— from my father to do so.

(2) Tom may ——— a book from his brother and
——— his own to you.

(3) I have ——— my pencil.   May I ——— one
from you, please?

2. **Funny, strange.**   Say:

The dog's tricks were so **funny** that every one laughed.
The dog's bark was so **strange** that his master knew
something was wrong.

In speaking of that which may cause a laugh, use the
word *funny*.   In speaking of that which causes a surprise, use the word *strange*.

(1) The monkey that performed many *funny* tricks
wore a ——— costume.

(2) The men wore daggers in their belts.   This seemed
——— to me.

(3) The poor old man looked ———.

3. **Learn, teach.**   Say:

I have **learned** to skate.   My brother **taught** me.

A person *learns* lessons, but he *teaches* people.   Never
use *learned* in such a sentence as *My brother taught me
how to skate*.

(1) Mary has *learned* to cook.   Her mother ———
her.

(2) John has *learned* how to use skis.   His father
——— him.

(3) The boys' teacher ——— them how to set type.

(4) Robert ——— his brother how to ride a bicycle.

(5) After Ruth had learned how to skate, she ———
her sister.

(6) John ——— his brother how to swim after he
himself had ——— how.

4. **Laying, lying.**   Say:

One scout is **laying sticks** on the fire.   The other scouts are **lying** on the ground.

The word *lying* is a form of the verb *lie*, meaning to recline.   It is correct to say *John lies on the couch*, *John is lying on the couch*, *John lay on the couch*, and *John has lain on the couch*.   The word *laying* differs from the word *lying* in that it takes the name of an object after it such as box, paper, or book.

(1) Bricks were *lying* on the ground.   Men were ———— bricks.

(2) The children were *lying* in their cribs.   The nurse was ———— a quilt over them.

(3) The boys were ———— on the grass in front of their tents.

(4) The blindman's dog was ———— near him.

(5) Mary was ———— in a hammock.   Helen was ———— her doll in a crib.

(6) The cat is ———— under the stove.

(7) Dick's hat is ———— on the table.

(8) Alice's pencil is ———— on the floor.

(9) The paper was ———— on the desk.   Helen was ———— paper on the shelf.

5. **Most, almost.**   Say:

Most boys like to play baseball.   **Almost** all of them play ball often.   Do not use *most* for *almost*.

(1) *Most* girls like outdoor sports.   ———— every girl in our class can skate.

(2) ———— all of the children in our school try to be prompt.

(3) I sent a valentine to ———— every one in my class.

6. **Real, very.**   Say:

This fur is **real** sealskin.   It is **very** soft.

Real means genuine.   It should never be used in place of *very* or *really*.   Maple sugar may be *real* maple sugar and *very* sweet.   Never say *real sweet, real good, real kind*, or *real well*.

(1) This is a *real* diamond.   It is ———— brilliant.

(2) John is a *real* boy.   He is ———— lively.

(3) I like candy ———— well.

(4) The lace was *real* lace.   It was ———— fine.

(5) The flowers were ———— pretty.

(6) Tom does not feel ———— well.

(7) The day was a ———— summer day.   It was ———— warm.

Test I.   Practice Exercises.   Telling what Happened

These Practice Exercises will be found on pages 270–274.

Test J.   Practice Exercises.   Speaking of One or More

Is, are; was, were.   Use **is** and **was** with singular subjects and **are** and **were** with plural subjects.

a. Notice that in each of the following cases the subject is singular.

> Either Mary or Helen **is** to go.
> Neither Tom nor his brother **is** at school.
> Each one of the boys **was** busy.
> Every one of the girls **has** her work finished.

b. Decide which of the following expressions, if it were used as a subject, would take a singular verb:

> The boys on the team   Either Fred or Tom
> Neither child   Every one in the class
> Both children   All of the children
> Each of the cousins   Neither he nor she

c. Use each expression in Exercise b as the subject of a statement containing the verb *is*, *are*, *was*, or *were*.

> Ex.: The boys on the team *were* ready for the game.

d. Review the exercises on pages 210 and 211.

For the use of *has*, *have*, *doesn't*, *don't*, and for other uses of *is*, *are*, *was*, and *were*, see pages 274–276.

Test K. Practice Exercises. Avoiding Senseless Expressions

1. **Words repeating the sense of other words.** Do not use a word that repeats the sense of some other word in the sentence. Say:

> **Alike;** not *both alike.*
> **Beginners;** not *new beginners.*

Connected; not *connected together.*
A pass; not *a free pass.*
Elevated; not *elevated up.*
Opened; not *opened up.*
Repeated; not *repeated over again.*

2. **Unnecessary words.** Omit unnecessary words.

Say:

Has (to show possession); not *has got.*
Behind; not *in back of.*
A kind of fruit; not *a kind of a fruit.*
A sort of vegetable; not *a sort of a vegetable.*
Take hold; not *take a hold.*
Beside; not *a side of* or *alongside of.*

3. **Have, could have, would have.** Pronounce *have* carefully; do not call it *half, of,* or *a.*

Say:

I have to leave; not *I half to* leave.
I could have gone; not *I could of gone* or *I could a gone.*
I should have known; not *I should of known* or *I should a known.*
I would have helped; not *I would of helped,* or *I would a helped.*

4. **Ought not.** Do not use *hadn't ought* for *ought not.*

Say: **I ought not** to go; or **I oughtn't** to go; not *I hadn't ought to go.*

a. Complete:

I *ought* to tell the truth.   I ——— not to tell a falsehood.
I *ought* to be kind.   I ——— not to be unkind.

b. Give an "ought not" for each of the following statements:

(1) I ought to be prompt.
(2) I ought to be orderly.
(3) I ought to be industrious.
(4) I ought to be courteous.
(5) I ought to speak good English.
(6) I ought to keep in good health.
(7) I ought to be ambitious.
(8) I ought to be thoughtful.

5. Like, as if. Say:

The man looked **like** a coward. He ran **as if** he were frightened.

Like may be used with a noun. *As if* is used in a comparison containing a verb. Do not use *like* in place of *as if*.

Use in sentences:

like a brave soldier   as if he enjoyed it
like an ambitious boy   as if she were in a hurry
like a good player   as if she were busy

6. Yet. Say:

The sun has not risen **yet.**

The word *yet* may be used with a verb preceded by *have*, *has*, and *had*, but not with the verb *did*. Do not say, *The sun did not rise yet.*

Test L.   Practice Exercises.   The Use of Adjectives and Adverbs

Any one making an error in Test L should use the exercises on pages 224 and 238 to help him avoid it.

SUMMARIES

1. Composing a Talk

Giving directions. See that you have a clear understanding of your subject. Plan the directions in such a way that a listener can get a clear idea of what is to be accomplished and just how it is to be done. Arrange your facts in order and express them as briefly as possible. Make every reference clear. Do not, for example, use the words *they* and *it* before you have mentioned that for which the words stand.

Making a report. Limit your subject to what can be covered in the time allotted. Remember that it is better to say much about a few points than to say a little about each of many points. Give your report with an outline in mind and with a very definite idea as to what you will say about each of the main topics. Do not try to repeat exactly what you have heard or read. Make the thought your own before you try to express it.

Telling a story. Select as a subject some event about which your listeners will be glad to hear. Plan what you have to say so that it will form a connected story that grows more and more interesting as it proceeds. Choose a beginning that arouses the interest of your listeners and helps them to understand what is coming; then keep the story moving. Tell enough facts to make the point clear, but do not put in parts of other stories. See that the ending brings the story to a definite conclusion. As you tell the story, try to express it in interesting sentences that are clear in meaning.   Try also to use words that help your audience to picture what you have in mind.

2. Giving a Talk

Face your audience before you begin to speak. Stand firmly on both feet in an easy, quiet position. Use a pleasant, low voice, but speak so distinctly that every one can hear you with ease.   Make your talk interesting and have it well in mind so that you can give it without hesitation and in a way that will show that you believe in what you are saying.

3. Listening to a Talk

Look in the direction of the speaker and encourage him by giving close attention to what he says. As he talks, compare your ideas with his.   Perhaps later you may be able to add something to the subject.   If any one needs help, be ready to give it in a courteous way.   Tell a speaker *what to do* rather than *what not to do*.   Avoid any appearance of finding fault.

4. Making a Paper Look Neat

To make a paper look neat, be careful to keep the margins even and to space it in such a way that no words are crowded.

Write your name in the upper right-hand corner.

So place the title of the paper that the space at the right and the one at the left are about equal. Leave an empty line above the title and another one below it.

```
GRADE                NAME

        TITLE OF PAPER

     _____

     _____
     _____
     _____
     _____
     _____
     _____

     _____
     _____
     _____
     _____
     _____
```

Make the left-hand margin an inch wide and the right-hand margin a half-inch wide.

Set in the first line of each paragraph about half an inch from the margin. Leave a space between sentences equal to the width of the letter *m*.

See that the margin at the bottom matches the right-hand margin.

5. Dividing a Word at the End of a Line

In dividing a word at the end of a line, see that the break comes between two syllables. Divide *Monday* in this way *Mon - day; beginning* thus *beginning*. Do not divide words of one syllable, such as *taught, through, laughed*. Avoid also dividing a word so that a syllable of one letter is separated from the rest of the word. Do not divide such words as *among, any, over, idle*.

6. Correcting Errors

Form the habit of looking through all written work after completing it.

See that all papers are written in separate and complete sentences without unnecessary *and's*.

With the help of the rules below and on page 293, make sure that capital letters are used where they are needed and that the paper is correctly punctuated.

Use the list of words on page 301 and your dictionary to help you with the spelling.

Be careful never to let an error in the use of words go uncorrected (see pages 6 and 263 for lists of common errors.)

If you find an error in a paper, correct it.   If the paper is written in pencil, erase the error without smudging the paper, and substitute the correct form. If it is written in ink, draw a line carefully through the error and write the correct form above it.   Use this method:

lightning   the

The tree was struck by ~~lightening~~ during ʌ night.

7. Rules for the Use of Capital Letters

Begin with a capital letter:

The first word of a sentence.

All proper names and all abbreviations for them.

All titles of respect and their abbreviations.

The word *God* and all other sacred names.

The first word and all other important words in the title of a book or story.

The first word in each line of poetry.

The first word of words quoted.

The first word of the greeting in a letter and the first word of the ending.

Write the words *I* and *O* as capitals.

Write as capitals the initials used in a proper name and those standing for the points of the compass.

8. Rules of Punctuation

Use a period:

At the end of each sentence that states a fact or gives a command.

After an abbreviation or an initial.

Use a question mark at the end of a question.

Use an exclamation point after a word or sentence showing surprise or other strong emotion.

Use a comma:

To separate the parts of a date.

To separate the parts of an address.

To set off words quoted.

To set off such words as *yes*, *no*, and *please*, when they are used independently in answering questions or making requests.

After both the greeting and the complimentary ending of a letter.

To set off the name of a person addressed or a word used in place of it.

To separate words in a list.

To separate the statements in a long sentence.

To set off words in a sentence that are used to explain others.

To set off at the beginning of a sentence the part introduced by *if*, *when*, *although*, and *because*.

9. Letter Form

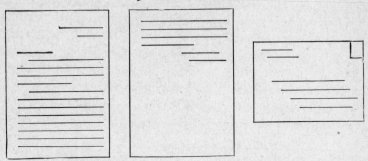

The spacing of a letter depends upon the size of the paper used, but for most letters the rules given here may be followed:

Leave a margin about an inch and a half wide at the top of the first page. Make the left-hand margin about half an inch wide and the right-hand one a quarter of an inch wide. Leave at the bottom a margin of the same width as the left-hand margin. The margin at the top of the second page and all succeeding pages should also match the left-hand margin.

Begin the date line below the address, half an inch to the right.

Indent (set in) the first word of each paragraph about half an inch.

In closing the letter, begin such words as *Sincerely yours*, *With love* at a point halfway across the page. Place your signature beneath the closing words half an inch farther to the right.

10. Addressing an Envelope

Avoid crowding the name and address on an envelope. Write the first line a little above the middle of the envelope. Make the space at the left and the one at the right about equal. Place the beginning of each new line half an inch farther to the right than the one directly above it. See that the lines form a series of even steps at the left.

Write your name and return address either in the upper left-hand corner or on the flap of the envelope at the back.

11. A Sixth Grade Composition Score

In measuring a composition, try to answer the following questions; then compare it with the compositions on pages 296, 297, 298, and 299.

Questions

Subject. Is the subject an interesting one? Is it limited to a topic that can be covered in the time allowed, or does it include too much? Has enough thought been given to it?

Plan. Does the composition form a connected story about one point or event, or is it a mere list of facts? Is enough said to make the point clear? Do all parts of the composition belong to the same story? Does the main point receive the most emphasis, or is too much made of the introduction or of some minor point?

Interest. Does the beginning of the story help you to understand what follows? Does the story grow more and more interesting as it proceeds? Is the ending a good one?

Use of sentences. Is the story told in separate and complete sentences? Are the sentences clear in meaning? Do they show variety in form and for that reason sound natural?

Use of words. Are all the words correctly used? Do they express what was intended? Do they seem appropriate? Are all unpleasant repetitions of the same word avoided?

Note: The following compositions should be marked *poor* unless they have redeeming traits: (1) all stories that are mixed up or that seem careless or foolish; (2) all long drawn-out accounts that have no point to them; (3) all papers that are too brief to be clear; (4) all stories that are told in "run-on" sentences; (5) all compositions that contain a number of errors in spelling, capitalization, punctuation, or in the use of words.

The following composition is *fair*.

VISITING THE ZOO

One day the family started for New York by auto. We went over the Mohawk Trail and planned to visit the zoo in Bronx Park.

We saw birds. One of them came on my shoulder and pecked me with its bill. I gave it some bread crumbs which it ate very quickly. The parrots talked with me. When I left for the hotel the birds were all asleep. The men said they went to sleep very early. It was only six o'clock.

Joseph

Although Joseph's paper contains some interesting facts, it fails to be good. The story is somewhat disconnected and many of the sentences sound abrupt.

The following compositions are *good*.

ALLIGATORS IN THE TOMOKA RIVER

One bright morning in March I left the dock at Daytona, Florida, in a large motor-boat which was to take

a party of us on a trip up the Tomoka River.   People said that on the banks of the river was a fine place
to see alligators.   We found this to be true soon after
the boat left the dock.   We counted sixty-six of them
all told on the trip up, and saw so many turtles that
we had to give up counting them.   On the trip home
we saw only forty-seven alligators for the sun had
gone down and it was too cold for them to stay out of
the water.

Carol

Carol's story is a simple, straightforward account
of an interesting experience.

THE KENTUCKY CARDINAL

One afternoon as I was bringing in the milk, I heard
a voice call, "What cheer, What cheer."   As I looked
up into the large sycamore tree above my head, I saw
a flash of red.   It was the Kentucky cardinal.

In a few moments there came to the same limb another bird, though not of the same vivid color.   It
was more of a brownish red.   I at once realized that
these two birds were mates.   They chattered and sang
in bird language which I thought was very comical.

Robert

In *The Kentucky Cardinal* Robert has confined his
story to a single brief incident, and in telling it he
has included a number of interesting and characteristic details.   Notice also that he has given variety
to his sentences and has used many picture-making
words such as "a *flash* of color," "*brownish* red,"
"the birds *chattered* and sang."

The following compositions are *excellent*.

AN ADVENTURE WITH A BEAR

Last summer when in Nova Scotia I went on a blue-
berrying trip.   We started in the morning in a large

covered wagon and after riding several miles into the woods, we decided to stop at a little clearing near a lake. We had our lunch with us for we planned to stay all day.

After picking all the morning we returned to the wagon about noon for our lunch. Just as we were arriving, one of the boys happened to see a brown furry animal coming out of the woods. As it started to come nearer, we saw that it was a large bear. One of the boys ran to the wagon to get a gun. He fired two or three shots, and the animal fell down as if dead. We were not anxious to meet any of the bear's relatives and so we decided to leave for home. As there was not room for the bear in the wagon and we did not exactly want him with us, two or three men said that they would return in another wagon to get him.

When we again reached the spot where the bear had fallen, to our surprise no bear was to be seen. Mr. Bear had fooled us and only played dead. However, he had given us an exciting day.

Charles

An Adventure with a Bear is a story told in an effective way: the introduction prepares the reader for what is coming; the story increases in interest as it proceeds; the conclusion brings the story to a definite end; the sentences used show enough variety to sound natural; and the words are well chosen.

GETTING READY TO DIE

One summer my cousin and I went strawberrying. Just about as fast as we picked the berries we would eat them.

Suddenly my cousin stopped and stared at me. "Oh," he said, "now you're going to die. You ate a worm on that strawberry."

I was so frightened I ran all the way home. When

I reached home I lay down on the couch. I said to myself, "Now, if I die, I'll not fall over and hurt myself." I waited a long, long time. Finally I fell asleep. When it was time for supper my mother came in and woke me. I looked at her in amazement and surprise. Then I said, "Haven't I died yet?"

Arline

Getting Ready to Die makes an interesting story not only because it is about an unusual subject, but because it works up to a climax and is humorous. Notice also that the conversation included helps to make the story a lively one.

12. Sixth Grade Program for Individual Progress in Form Study and Correct Usage

Unit No. 1

1. Twelve Common Errors, pp. 139–140. Test G.

2. Practice Exercises for Test G, pp. 281–282.

3. Recognizing a Sentence, p. 142, Ex. 4.

4. Review, Use of Capitals, p. 144, Ex. 1, 2, 3.

5. Marks of Punctuation, p. 144, Ex. 4, 5, 6, 7, 8.

6. Mastery of the Sentence, Test No. 1, pp. 145–146.

Unit No. 2

1. Proof-Reading — The Comma, p. 158, Ex. 4, 5, 6.

2. Surnames, p. 160, Ex. 1; p. 161, Ex. 2, 3, 4.

3. Nouns, p. 161, Ex. 5, 6, 7 (continued on page 162).

4. Common and Proper Nouns, p. 162, Ex. 8, 9, 10; p. 163, Ex. 11, 12, 13, 14, 15, 16.

5. Review, Plurals and Possessives, p. 163, Ex. 17; p. 164, Ex. 18, 19.

6. Using Words Correctly, p. 164, Test H.

7. Practice Exercises for Test H, pp. 282–285.

Unit No. 3

1. Proof-Reading — Paragraphing, p. 178, Ex. 4.

2. Words Needed in Stating a Fact:

Verbs Expressing Action, p. 179, Ex. 1, 2; p. 180, Ex. 3, 4, 5.

Verbs Used in Describing a Condition, p. 180, Ex. 6, 7; p. 181, Ex. 8, 9, 10.

3. Combining Ideas in a Sentence, p. 254, Ex. 1, 2, 3, 4; p. 255, Ex. 5.

4. Summary. The Parts of Speech, p. 256, Ex. 1, 2; p. 257, Ex 3.

5. Mastery of the Sentence. Test No. 3, pp. 258–259.

6. Using Words Correctly, pp. 260–262. Tests J, K, L.

7. Practice Exercises for Tests J, K, L, p. 285–288.

13. One Hundred Spelling Demons

COMPILED BY DR. W. FRANKLIN JONES

ache	done	making	they
again	don't	many	though
always	early	meant	through
among	easy	minute)	tired
answer	enough	much	to-night
any	every	none	trouble
been	February	often	truly
beginning	forty	once	Tuesday
believe	friend	piece	two
blue	grammar	raise	too
break	guess	read (red)	used
built	half	ready	very
busy	having	said	wear
business	hear	says	Wednesday
buy	heard	seems	week
can't	here	separate	where
choose	hour	shoes	whether
color	hoarse	since	which
coming	instead	some	whole
could	just	straight	women
cough	knew	sugar	won't
country	know	sure	would
dear	laid	tear	write
doctor	loose	their	writing
does	lose	there	wrote

Used by permission of Hall & McCreary Company, Chicago.

INDEX